TAMING
the *Lecture Bug*

and Getting Your Kids to Think

JOEY AND CARLA LINK

PRESS

Taming the Lecture Bug
and Getting Your Kids to Think
by Joey and Carla Link

Printed in the United States of America.

ISBN 9781498435857

www.xulonpress.com

Praise for

Taming the Lecture Bug
and
Getting Your Kids to Think

"Direct, simple, thoughtful and engaging! These are words that only begin to describe this practical, easy reading conversation that is "Taming the Lecture Bug". More than a training manual or self-help child behavior book asserting what parents need to do to insure good behavior in their children; the authors encourage and equip parents, counselors, and anyone caring about the development of children to deal with root behavioral issues. While the truths are biblically based, the topics covered make this a helpful tool for any parent training their pre-adult children for future success in higher education."

– Brett Smith
Educator, Counselor and University Administrator *(retired)*
California State University, San Francisco

"As President of Global Operations for a global medical manufacturer and distributor, we developed detailed standard operating procedures so our thousands of team members know exactly how to handle every aspect of their job in a manner that will exceed our customers' expectations. In this book, our good friends Joey and Carla have developed a biblical standard operating procedure to combat the most common parenting approach–lecturing. Joey and Carla's wisdom and biblical approach to parenting have been invaluable to Joan and I as we are raising our five children."

– B. Abington
EVP & President of Global Operations
Global Medical Manufacturer and Distributor

"Christian children are faced with competing worldviews, ideas and beliefs antithetical to the Bible, more so today than at any other time in recent history. The current ineffectiveness of the Church to reach and keep young people for Christ can clearly be traced back to parents' inability to teach and train their children to think logically and biblically for themselves. Joey and Carla's **Taming the Lecture Bug** is a must have for every Christian parent who wants to raise responsible children to see them own their faith, grow their faith and maintain their faith into and throughout adulthood."

Ivo "Trey" Roberts
Associate Pastor, White Dove Fellowship
Ministry of Christian Education
New Orleans, LA

Table of Contents

Dedication

To Gary and Anne Marie
Thank you for investing in us all those years ago
and implanting your biblical teaching into our hearts.
May we be found faithful.

Acknowledgements

*F*irst and most importantly, we want to thank our Lord and Savior, Jesus Christ for considering us worthy to serve Him by ministering to families. It is a privilege we do not take lightly.

Many of the foundational principles shared in this book are based on teaching in the Growing Families Int'l parenting curricula and are used with the permission and blessing of the authors.

We want to thank our children for allowing us to use stories of their growing up years throughout our teaching and this book.

We are grateful to our daughter, Amy Carpenter for her assistance on any project we throw her way, but especially for her photography work seen on the cover of the book and our photograph. She is the principal photographer for Refuge Studios in Nashville, TN.

We have known most of you who gave the endorsements on the back cover of the book and testimonials at the end of each chapter for many years now. We are well acquainted with your children and have seen the fruit of your parenting efforts. Thank you for allowing us to be a part of your families.

We want to give a special acknowledgement to Steve and Lesli Murphy who allowed us to share a story about their daughter which became the core teaching in Chapter 7. They just started using the teaching we share in this book a couple years ago with their teenagers, and they inspire us with their commitment to succeed at seeing their kids' hearts become God-trained.

Finally, to all of you across the globe who have trusted us to assist you in raising your children through our teaching, counseling, Mom's Notes presentations, books and DVDs — thank you for the privilege and honor of serving you. We are grateful.

Introduction

At one time or another, every parent lectures their kids, usually in frustration and anger. Why do parents keep lecturing their kids when they don't change their behavior? What lecture has made your child clean his room, put his clothes away, do his chores or get his homework done? He might do it for the moment because your tone of voice tells him you are imagining every worst case scenario possible for him if he doesn't, but will he feed the dog tomorrow? Parents lecture because they don't know what else to do to motivate their kids to get their stuff done.

To make sure we are all on the same page as far as parenting is concerned, constant reminders, threats, and lectures don't work. What else can you do? This book will give you practical tools used by parents all over the world to motivate kids to change their behavior and take ownership of their daily life responsibilities.

We will be encouraging you to look at the reasons why your kids are irresponsible from a different perspective. We want you to enjoy your kids and teens without running around trying to figure out which of their chores or schoolwork they haven't completed yet.

To keep things simple, we have used the pronoun "he" to represent children in the text. The information in this book is by no means gender specific. We don't want you to get the impression we think only boys are irresponsible.

We often use the word "child" to represent all children at every age. If a comment is age-specific, it is mentioned in the text.

Study questions for each chapter of this book can be downloaded at www.parentingmadepractical.com. Churches and small groups alike found the study questions helpful as they went through our previous book, *"Why Can't I Get My Kids to Behave?"* in groups.

Parents can get more teaching through blog posts along with recommended resources for all ages on our website www.parentingmadepractical.com.

Joey & Carla Link

Chapter 1

Blah, Blah, Blah...

*T*he laundry was folded and ready to be put away. Like usual, the baskets of folded clothes were placed at the foot of the stairs. Each of our children had their own basket and it was their job to pick up their basket, take it to their room and put their clothes away in their dresser drawers.

Seems simple enough, right? A couple hours later, as I (Carla) was headed upstairs, I noticed our son's basket still on the floor by the steps. I knew he had made several trips up the stairs, so I was not happy with this discovery. When I walked by the girls' room, I looked in and saw Amy's clothes were stacked neatly in a pile on her bed. I wondered why on earth she couldn't have taken the time to put them in the drawers where they belonged.

"Not happy" was an understatement for how I felt when I looked at Briana's side of the room and noticed her clothes had been dumped on the floor by her bed. As I was furiously yelling their names, I thought for the zillionth time, "How many times have I told them...?" This was hardly a new situation in our home.

Once I had the attention of all three of my children (late elementary and middle school age), I started in on an angry lecture they had heard dozens of times before. I was sure my tone of voice let them know I was serious and they better not do this to my hard work again. They would put the clothes away where they belonged next time, or else!

Seeing how upset I was, Amy assured me she was going to clean out her drawers later and fold the clothes neatly and put them all away. Her drawers were too messy to add the nicely folded clothes I had put in her basket, she explained. Briana just shrugged and said she didn't know why she hadn't taken the time to put her clothes away, but after dumping them on the floor, she put the empty basket in her closet where it belonged. She was sure this would impress me.

In a tone that told me he knew everything and I knew nothing, Michael let me know he didn't see the basket at the bottom of the stairs (he would have had to trip over it) and admitted he wouldn't have put his clothes away if he had seen it. He thought putting them in the dresser was an unnecessary chore when it was easier to pull what he wanted to wear out of the basket when it was in the middle of the room. I really didn't get how that would be easier than pulling them out of a drawer, and told him so.

My head and my heart were doing a battle of their own. On one hand, I knew no one else cared if he put his laundry away so why should I? On the other hand, I worried if I let this go, what would he decide he didn't have to do my way next? If I didn't require him to follow through with simple tasks and responsibilities like putting his laundry away, then what kind of an employee would he be as an adult? Would he tell his employer he was going to do a task the way he thought best rather than the way his boss told him to do it?

I was tired of fighting with him and just wanted peace and no conflict. I finally decided when Michael knew he had won, he would continue to take control by choosing to do more things his way, and I could not let that happen.

Don't Give Your Authority Away

Whoever is in control has authority over the people under him. Michael already spent his time trying to take our authority away from us, so we surely weren't going to hand it to him on a silver platter. I pulled myself together, and in a calm tone, I launched into the lecture to end all lectures. Midway through, I noticed Michael looking at the door, plotting his escape. The girls were quietly sitting on their beds, nodding their heads in agreement to whatever I was saying.

In utter despair, I realized none of them were paying attention to a word I was saying; "blah, blah, blah" was all they were hearing. They were all waiting until I was done, at which time they would tell me they would put their clothes away next time and get away from me as fast as it was humanly possible to do so.

The next week, the same thing happened again. Amy, being our non-conflict child, got her clothes put away nicely, but Briana and Michael were another story. Briana left her basket on her bed and arranged pillows in front of it and Michael shoved his clean, folded clothes under his bed. I was pretty sure this could not be considered progress. In an angrier tone of voice, the same lecture popped out of my mouth before I could stop it.

Why, oh why don't our kids get it? As much as I stewed on this when our kids were growing up, I also knew I did the same thing when I was a kid. If I didn't want to do what I was told to do, I did everything I could to get out of doing it. I surely don't remember the "why" behind this thinking. Wouldn't it be easier to just do the task than to put up with parents with fire coming out of their mouths?

Tweaking the Standard

Our children were taking what we told them to do and tweaking it ever so slightly, distorting the standards we set. Let's go back to the laundry. One week I found Michael's laundry dumped in a pile on his desk. After hearing my lecture once again, Michael said, "You told me to put it away and I did. I decided where you see it is 'put away.'"

Ready to throttle him, I started yelling because he knew *exactly* what "put away" really meant. During the weeks and months of the laundry showing up anywhere but "away", I remember Briana putting her basket of clean, folded clothes in her closet, telling me she decided they should stay there until she had time to put them away properly. She evidently didn't have time to put them away at all, because when I did the laundry the next week, I found her dirty clothes thrown on top of the clean, folded ones.

I walked into the girls' room another time and found Amy's laundry in neat piles on her bed, where she determined they would stay until she had chosen what clothes she wanted to wear that week.

Our kids were little by little, changing our standards in front of our eyes, and we weren't catching on. Soon the "little by little" became "bigger and uglier" and they were changing the standard in other areas as well. Reminding turned into nagging, nagging turned into a full-blown lecture which turned into a yelling match.

What Lectures Don't Do

Lecturing is just a polite way of yelling at your kids for not getting something done or for not doing it right.

When parents lecture, they think they are helping their children by reminding them of the training and teaching they have given them. Lecturing is just a polite way of yelling at your kids for not getting something done or for not doing it right. This is what lectures ***don't*** do:

➢ **Lectures do not give kids new information**. When was the last time a lecture you gave one of your kids told him something he didn't already know? When your kids already know what they are supposed to do, the last thing they want is to hear you tell them why they should do it.

➢ **Lectures do not motivate kids to do the right thing**. When you are lectured by your spouse, parent, or your employer, does it motivate you to do the right thing? Then why do we think lecturing our kids is going to accomplish this? Lectures are just words that truly go in one ear and out the other.

➢ **Lectures do not encourage kids to succeed**. Pointing out what your kids did wrong makes them feel like failures, and they lose confidence in their ability to do anything right. After getting another lecture from me (Carla), one of my daughters once asked me in utter despair if I could point out one thing she did right. I might have been giving her encouragement or words of praise along the way, but what she told me on that day with this question was the negative (lectures) far outweighed the positive (praise and encouragement).

> ➢ **Lectures do not give kids (especially teens) the freedom to make mistakes they can learn from**. The lessons we learn from poor choices are memorable. Giving your kids the freedom to fail when they are living in your home teaches them how to deal with failure when they will one day live on their own. Giving them the freedom to fail doesn't mean they will get away with the behavior, it means you work with them to find a way to succeed the next time around.

Wasted Breath

As we shared in the laundry story, when Carla and I lectured our kids, all they heard was "blah, blah, blah" and nothing else. Kids aren't listening to you when you lecture, so you are just wasting words and breath.

Pointing out what your kids did wrong makes them feel like failures, and they lose confidence in their ability to do anything right.

Noted teacher and Bible expositor Chuck Swindoll has this to say about listening when others are talking:

"Research at the University of Minnesota reveals that in listening to a ten-minute talk, hearers operate at only a twenty-eight percent efficiency. And the longer the talk, the less we understand, the less we track with our ears what somebody's mouth is saying."[1]

When you lecture, your kids are unengaged because they know nothing is required of them. Kids keep a small sliver of their mind tuned in to what their parent is saying and let the other part of their mind wander wherever it wants to go. It is depressing to realize our kids don't have to think hard about what we are saying to keep track of our words and intent, isn't it?

Why Do Parents Lecture?

If lectures don't make kids change their behavior, then why do we lecture them when we know it isn't going to work?

When you lecture, your kids are unengaged because they know nothing is required of them.

It is easy to lecture your kids because:

- It doesn't take a lot of time
- Lectures can be given anywhere (you can lecture your kids in the car if you need to go somewhere)
- Lectures help parents feel better because it allows them to let off steam

When my kids were teens and I needed to let them have it, I (Carla) would tell them I had a good lecture in me and they were going to hear it. They were going to nod their heads in agreement to what I was saying and when I was finished they were going to do what I told them to do and smile while they were at it!

The following are more reasons parents resort to lecturing:

➢ **Bad Experience**–Like our laundry story, you are certain your kids aren't going to do what they said they would do because history does repeat itself, so you think you have to keep reminding them to get it done right. What are you teaching your kids when they know they don't have to remember what they need to do because you are going to do all their "remembering" for them?

➢ **Expectations Not Met** – Your children didn't follow through on what they said they would do and your expectations were dashed once again. You are worried they will not ever reach their potential to be fine, upstanding young men and women one day. You continue to lecture and remind them, hoping they will grow into responsible and mature adults.

➢ **Unwise Choices** – Parents are so sure their child will not make a wise choice they start lecturing him before he has the opportunity to prove them wrong. Once the lecture is over, your child decides to prove you right, and another unwise choice ensues.

➢ **Legalism–**The legalistic parent always fears the worst. They fence their children in with their lectures and reminders. They think they are helping their children by pointing out the potential problems that could arise in an effort to stop their kids from failing. Quite the opposite is true however, for lectures stop kids from succeeding.

Ultimately, parents lecture because they want their kids to be responsible. Children and teens choose to be irresponsible, disobedient, and rebellious to how they have been taught to live and act despite their parent's best efforts.

How Parents Lecture
How do you lecture your kids? These are the ways most parents use:

- Reminding
- Threatening
- Talking over your kids when they are talking
- Talking without first getting your kids attention
- Nagging
- Debating
- Negotiating

Well, these don't sound appealing, do they? We want you to know you can stop lecturing. It is going to take work to break this bad habit. I (Joey) would walk out of the room when I felt a lecture coming on so I would resist the temptation to let my kids have it. You could see Carla's mouth clamped shut when she was trying to hold the lecture in. With time and effort, we tamed the lecture bug in our house, and you can too! So, what can you do to turn this around?

Obedience Comes First

From our perspective, to "turn this around" means children are going to obey their parents "immediately, completely, without arguing or complaining." [2] If you want more information on training your kids to obey, you will find it in our book, "*Why Can't I Get My Kids to Behave?*"

Carla had shown the kids how she wanted the laundry put away, neatly, in their drawers. For them to change this instruction on their own, without first asking permission is not just about disobeying their mother, it is about determining the character of who they are going to become as they grow and mature. When they re-wrote the definition of "put away", they re-wrote the definition of "obedience" as well.

If one of the kids couldn't get their laundry put away when Carla told them to, all this child had to do was say, "Mom, I don't have time to put my laundry away right now. May I do it later? I will have it done before I go to bed."

What do you think their mom would have said? So, how did it get to the point where our kids didn't care where they put their laundry and they couldn't take a few seconds to ask for permission to put it away later? They were getting plenty of reminders and lectures. They were even getting consequences. I remember laundry baskets in our room filled with "not-put-away" clothes. If they didn't get them put away correctly, Carla would confiscate the clothes until they started putting the laundry away the right way.

When Carla backed off, they backed off and the laundry didn't get put away once again. Carla cleaned out their drawers, thinking there were too many clothes in them to fit the clean ones in. Yet the laundry still did not get put away.

When the consequences didn't work, Carla would fall back on lecturing, the good old standby. Or, she would bring me into the picture and I would do the lecturing for her. When lectures become the only consequence kids receive, we learned the hard way a lecture isn't painful enough to cause a kid to change his behavior.

We thought our kids obeyed us. If you asked us during the weeks and months of the "laundry problem", we would have told you our kids obeyed when we said to (immediately), how we said to (completely), with no arguing or complaining. And they were obeying this way when it came to the big things. But when it came to the little things like putting their laundry away, their obedience training was tucked into the laundry basket that was stuck in the closet.

All of a Sudden

A couple approached us after a session we had just taught at a parenting conference. They shared with us how one of their children was misbehaving. In the middle of the story the parent said, "And all of a sudden, he started ..."

When relating a story about one of their children, parents often say this phrase. We want you to understand there is no such thing as "all of a sudden" when it comes to your kids' behavior. When kids don't obey in the little things,

> *When kids don't obey in the little things, they start the ball rolling and by the time it gets down the hill, it has become a big, ugly mass of rebellion.*

they start the ball rolling and by the time it gets down the hill, it has become a big, ugly mass of rebellion.

When we realized we needed to get this ball back up the hill and start requiring obedience in the "little" things, we started to see our kids hop to it around our house in other areas as well. So, despite wanting no conflict, despite being busy with other things, despite being tired of dealing with defiant kids, we took it on and our children learned to put the laundry away, our way.

Carla would tell the kids they could put it away any way they wanted when they lived on their own. When Briana went to college and we visited her there, she would always proudly take us to her dorm room and say, "See, my laundry is put away!"

We are going to encourage you and challenge you with what we learned in parenting our own children and in working with hundreds of parents across the globe. When you tame the lecture bug in your home, peace will come. We look forward to giving you tools to change your child's behavior in ways that will ultimately change his heart and exterminate that lecture bug out of your house!

But first, we need to lay a foundation of what needs to be in place before your kids will become responsible.

"The practical wisdom Joey and Carla have shared with us through the years about how not to lecture our kids has been an invaluable tool in our parenting. This makes life easier and more enjoyable for everyone, particularly in our unique situation with a dad who travels full time for work and a mom who deals with chronic pain. When they were very young, we established obedience with our children as talked about in this chapter. As our children grew older, we learned to ask them questions, helping them think through situations and problem solve in a logical way rather than giving a lecture. Learning to ask questions of our kids has saved them from many "blah, blah, blah" moments.

When I am having a bad day of pain and my husband is traveling, I am glad I don't have to remind and lecture my kids to complete their responsibilities. We often spend our evenings debriefing about the day and we are thankful for the mature ways they are able to think things through and the decisions they make on their own."

This teaching has been a priceless gift to our family, and we are excited about the tools that will be shared in this book. As we have consistently applied these principles, we have seen wonderful fruit in our children, who are now 18, 15 and 13."

-Don and Karen, Tennessee

*"My son, if you receive my words and treasure up my commandments with you,
making your ear attentive to wisdom and inclining your heart to understanding;
yes, if you call out for insight and raise your voice for understanding,
if you seek it like silver and search for it as for hidden treasures,
then you will understand the fear of the Lord and find the knowledge of God."*
Proverbs 2:1-5

Chapter 2

Why Aren't Kids Thinking?

*E*mma was driving home from school. Her family lived several miles out of town, and it took twenty minutes or so to get home. On this particular day, Emma decided to text on her cell phone with a friend she had just spent the day with at school. Busy texting, Emma missed a curve and went off the road and hit a tree. Thankfully, Emma didn't suffer major injuries. The same could not be said for the car.

Emma's parents had told her again and again not to text when she was driving. So why did Emma choose to disobey? First of all, all her friends texted on their cell phones when they were driving even though they were told not to by their parents, so why shouldn't she? She didn't initiate the text, she just picked up the phone when it buzzed, so she justified her lack of obedience using this excuse.

Frankly, being alone in the car, she didn't think she would get caught. But she did get caught, and in the most horrific way imaginable for any parent. But really, what adult, teen or child thinks the "worst case scenario" is ever going to happen to them?

In relating this story to us, Emma's mom said, "What was she thinking?! We have told her over and over again the cell phone is only for emergencies when she is driving. How can we trust her not to use the phone when she drives?"

What was she thinking? The problem is Emma chose **not** to think. When she heard the text come through she didn't think about her parents' rules regarding use of the phone in the car.

It never occurred to her not to pick it up, nor did it occur to her when she looked at the text that she was disobeying. She became so engrossed in texting back and forth with her friend she forgot to pay attention to her driving. Emma didn't think when she answered the text, she **reacted** and the price she paid was huge.

Why Don't Kids Think Before They Act?

When there is something questionable your kids want to do, they don't want to decide if it is right or wrong. If they take the time to think about why it could be wrong and what they should do instead, they would lose the enjoyment of doing it. It is better for them to act instead of think.

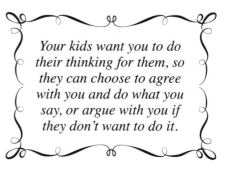

Your kids want you to do their thinking for them, so they can choose to agree with you and do what you say, or argue with you if they don't want to do it.

Reasons Why Kids Don't Want to Think:

1. **Thinking is too much work**. Your kids want you to do their thinking for them, so they can choose to agree with you and do what you say, or argue with you if they don't want to do it. As long as you are willing to do their thinking for them, the **less** responsible they have to be. It is easier for your kids to argue with you than it is for them to think about how to manage their own behavior in an appropriate way. Stop talking Mom and Dad. Stop nagging, stop reminding, and stop lecturing. Make your kids think for themselves.

2. **Kids have to deal with the ramifications of their actions when they think**. When you think for your kids, this makes them followers and you the leader. As the one who made the decision, you have to deal with the ramifications of their actions. Can't you hear it now? "But Mom, I was just doing what you told me to!"

3. **Kids feel overwhelmed when no one else is doing the right thing.** It is easier to go along with the crowd than stand alone. The crowd does the thinking and your child follows along. Peer pressure wins again. This is especially true when their friends in "the crowd" are Christians. In today's culture, including the Christian community, there isn't a common standard anymore. It's almost like it was in the book of Judges:

> *"In those days there was no king in Israel.*
> *Everyone did what was right in his own eyes."*
> Judges 21:25

There **is** a common standard however for all of us who believe in God, and it's called the Bible. It is the voice of God and it has never changed. God doesn't keep sending down rewrites or revisions. He got it right the first time. Therefore, what it says still applies to us today. It is the foundation we work off of for life and parenting. If the Bible is not your foundation, what is?

4. **Kids aren't thinking because they don't know the "why" or the "how".** Parents tell their kids what to do or what not to do, but they aren't teaching or training them **why** they should or should not do something or **how** they can avoid doing something that is wrong for them to do. When temptation raises its monstrous head, kids don't know *why* they need to resist it (other than their parents said to) or how to resist it so they do what seems right in the moment..

5. **Kids aren't held accountable for their actions.** Teaching kids what is right to do is one thing. To hold them accountable to do it is quite another. It is work, something busy parents often don't take the time to do. You find out your twelve year-old son didn't do his homework. He is playing on the computer instead. You are running out the door to

take his brother to soccer practice. What do you do? You give him a verbal thrashing (another way of saying you lecture him). Even then, you are not surprised when you get home to find his schoolwork has not been touched. Giving your kids a lecture is not holding them accountable for their actions. Reminding your kids is not holding them accountable for their actions. Giving your kids consequences is holding them accountable for their actions.

6. **Kids are self-focused**. When kids put more importance on what they want to do instead of what they need to do, doing the right thing becomes unimportant to them. Self-focused kids have too great an opinion of themselves and they think they know better than their parents or anyone else. They have too much knowledge and not enough experience, a dangerous combination which makes them proud and arrogant.

What Parents Can Do

Parents get caught up in lecturing their kids because they truly believe they are helping them. However, lectures don't get your kids to think for themselves. Neither do reminders, nagging, bribing or negotiating. More often than not, lectures turn your kids away from you.

The biggest thing parents can do to get their kids to think for themselves is to stop doing their thinking for them

If lectures don't work, what does? The biggest thing parents can do to get their kids to think for themselves is to stop doing their thinking for them.

"As parents, it is very easy to go into "lecture mode" where we vent all of our frustrations over a situation and our children endure the verbal lashing as we tell them how they should have handled something or what they should have said. However, this is not mutually beneficial. We have learned that we need to dialogue, not monologue with our children.

It works best if we think of questions that will cause our children to probe into their motives and see what they believe before we start the conversation with them. Our desire is that they will take ownership of their actions and the biblical principles we have put in their hearts as well. Our responsibility is to be proactive and not reactive. We have had to learn how to ask questions that engage our children to think for themselves. This is not easy and it takes work on our part, but the end result is well worth it.

One of our kids would be totally content if we did all of this child's thinking and made all the decisions, but this will not produce an adult who can make wise choices. We want our children to be able to stand up for themselves on their own two feet. Another child prefers to be argumentative and defensive whenever we enter into a dialogue. This is not healthy either because finding a way to blame the situation on others will not produce satisfying and lasting relationships.

With a healthy dialogue our children have learned to think for themselves and take ownership of each situation they encounter. In the long run, it's much easier to be on the same team when we are working with our children. We want them to confide in us and share their hearts but we have to be "emotionally safe" to earn this privilege. Lectures are humiliating for a child and they do not build trust.

Being the parents of three teenagers we want you to remember this – your kids will grow into young adults who will live life on their own. When that day comes, they need to be ready to make their own decisions, and if you've never required them to think for themselves, they won't be prepared to face the "real world".

Bryan and Dee, Oklahoma

"For wisdom will enter your heart,
and knowledge will be pleasant to your soul.
Discretion will protect you,
and understanding will guard you. "
Proverbs 2:10-11

Chapter 3

Ownership = Responsibility

*L*isa was talking with her friend Anne over lunch at their favorite restaurant. Report cards had just come out and Lisa was sharing how furious she and her husband were with their son Wyatt. Although a bright young man, he was barely passing his classes at the high school. They had contacted his teachers to find out why. They were told he rarely turned in his homework assignments, he hadn't turned in papers that were due and wasn't prepared when exam time came.

When they confronted Wyatt and asked him why he wasn't turning in his work, he told them school was boring and he had other things to do. His father was so angry Lisa thought the entire neighborhood could have heard him bellowing at their son. His dad unloaded a lecture to end all lectures to let Wyatt know in no uncertain terms he was destined to be a failure if he didn't pull himself together.

Lisa sighed deeply as she told Anne she didn't know what she was going to do with either of them. Her husband was determined to scream their son into submission and Lisa didn't think she could bear it. Wyatt still thought he would be able to get into college no matter what his grade point average, and they couldn't get it through his thick head his grades were the ticket he needed to get there.

Lisa told Anne how lucky she was her daughter Megan was getting good grades. On her way home, Anne couldn't get the conversation out of her mind. Being a single mom, she worried enough as it was if she was teaching her daughter all she needed to know before she was out on her own. Megan did get good grades, but the price Anne paid for them was wearing her out. She had to constantly stay on top of Megan's assignments to make sure she got them done, because Megan procrastinated and was always running around like a chicken with its head cut off trying to get her work turned in on time.

Despite countless reminders and lectures about staying on top of her schoolwork, nothing changed. That evening, Anne found herself at the public library getting research books for Megan so she could write a paper for her history class.

"Am I lucky?" Anne wondered. "I sure don't feel lucky in the middle of Megan's panic attacks when her assignments come due. Well, at least it isn't as bad as Lisa has it with Wyatt," she thought to herself.

When Megan came home from school the following day, she told her mom she had heard Wyatt complaining to his friends that he was going to have to get his schoolwork done to get his dad off his back. Anne told Megan how proud she was of her grades as she gave her a kiss on the cheek.

Be Responsible

Do you think kids who need reminders to get their stuff done are responsible? What about kids who do their chores, but never seem to do them the way they are supposed to be done? Are they being responsible?

The definition of the word, "responsible" is, "*able to respond or answer for one's conduct and obligations; trustworthy.*" [1]

Can Wyatt's parents trust him to get his homework done, do it right and get it turned in on time? What about Megan? Can she be trusted to get her work turned in on time without intervention from her mother? How about your children? Can you trust them to get their chores and schoolwork done without reminders and prompting from you?

Who's the Responsible One?

If you have to remind your kids (8-9 years and older) to get their chores and schoolwork done, you are the responsible one. If you have to check and make sure they did their assignments before they leave for school, you are the responsible one.

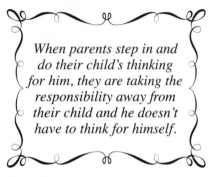

When kids think things through for themselves before they act, they are taking ownership of that behavior or action. When parents step in and do their child's thinking for him, they are taking the responsibility away from their child and he doesn't have to think for himself.

When parents step in and do their child's thinking for him, they are taking the responsibility away from their child and he doesn't have to think for himself.

When you put your child's thinking cap on your head and work through how he should behave, your child gets to sit back and relax, waiting for you to make the next move. When you tell him what he needs to do, he argues with you if he doesn't want to do it, wearing you down until you finally give in and let him do what he wants. We have seen this work for 2 year-olds (arguing for them is in the form of screaming and crying) through 20 year-olds.

Take the Thinking Cap Off

Beth was frustrated with her 14 year-old son Jake when she called one day. He was a good athlete and his team's best soccer player. All season long, he would forget something at home that he needed to play. Even though she had gotten him a bag to keep his gear in, something seemed to almost always get left at home. Often it was his shoes as he would get them out to play in the back yard with his friends and brothers.

Beth didn't want him to miss out on a game, plus she knew the team needed him to play, so she kept going back home (even though it was a twenty minute drive one way) to look for the forgotten soccer gear, as Jake knew she would. Beth needed to stop hovering over Jake, reminding him of every little detail to help him get and keep his stuff together. I (Joey) worked with her to come up with a new plan of action.

Jake needed to learn a valuable lesson. He was making his mom feel guilty when she complained about having to go back home; reminding her the team probably wouldn't win unless he played. Because he was refusing to check and make sure he had his gear before leaving the house however, he was holding his mom hostage in the process.

Before the next game, I recommended she remind him twice to get his gear together, which was significantly less than she had been doing. It was time to give the ownership of getting his gear together back to Jake. That afternoon as they were getting ready to go, Beth asked Jake one more time if he had everything he needed. He told his mom he did, again not checking his bag.

Get Eye Contact

One of the problems when reminding your kids is you usually call the reminder out to them wherever they may be. If you want your children to hear what you say with the intention of doing it, call their name and wait for them to come to you and look you in the eye.

Once you give an instruction (reminders are instructions) let your kids know you want them to give you a verbal response, indicating they heard what you said. Otherwise, when you ask them later why the task wasn't completed, they will often tell you they didn't hear you.

Jake's next game was a thirty minute drive across town. He walked to the field and opened his bag and was missing one of his soccer shoes. The first words out of his mouth were, "Mom, I can't find one of my soccer shoes." His mom suggested he check the car. He asked her to go do it for him. Beth shrugged and told him it wasn't her shoe that was missing so he needed to look for it himself.

Jake told his mom he had played soccer with his brothers in the back yard the day before, so he probably dropped the shoe in the grass when he went inside the house. She calmly told him if he had checked to make sure all his gear was in his bag, both his shoes would be there and he would be on the field warming up with the rest of the team.

As her son stood staring at her, Beth asked him who was responsible for his gear being in the bag. Jake ignored her question and tried putting a guilt trip on her, telling her how important this game was and how much the team needed him to play.

Kids Can Be Master Manipulators

Kids are good at using manipulation on their parents' emotions with their words, looks and actions. Wanting the best for their kids, parents usually give in like Beth had been doing with Jake. What Beth didn't realize, is she was training Jake not to be responsible all the while this young man was manipulating her to take the fall for his failure.

Bailing your kids out when they are unwilling to think things through for themselves is like mowing over a dandelion weed in your beautifully manicured lawn. All it does is drive the root deeper and it pops up again in a few days with stronger roots.

Like most moms, Beth wanted to help her son be the best he could be and was willing to do anything for him to accomplish this. Beth was assuming Jake was doing his part by remembering to check his gear before he left the house.

The first time Jake left a soccer shoe at home was an accident, but the eighth, ninth and tenth times? This was irresponsible behavior for this 7th grade boy. By going home more than half of Jake's games and practices to get something he needed to play, Beth was setting a pattern that became a habit. Jake didn't have to be responsible. His mom was on his team, doing a great job of playing back-up.

What Jake did not know yet was his mom was done mowing over this dandelion of irresponsible behavior. Beth had to work to keep her mouth quiet and not yell at him for once again forgetting to check his bag after she had reminded him. This would do nothing more than cause more frustration and separation between Beth and Jake emotionally. The time to address this is when the crisis is over and both Beth and Jake can talk logically and unemotionally.

You're On Your Own

When Jake finally realized his mom was not going to budge, he walked back to the bench discouraged. He couldn't believe his mom would not go get his shoe for him. One of Jake's teammates asked him why he wasn't on the field warming up. He told his teammate he left one of his shoes at home. Telling his friend he had left his shoe at home was a big first step for Jake, because he was not good at admitting he did something wrong.

When parents keep doing the thinking for their kids, they are training them to live in a world that is not real. What employer wants to hire someone who won't think on his own and is always running to him for advice or is not getting things done? Who wants to be married to a spouse who makes you do all his (or her) thinking and decision making? This creates a parent-child relationship instead of a husband-wife relationship, a concept that has been defined as co-dependent.

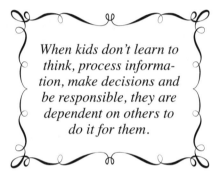

When kids don't learn to think, process information, make decisions and be responsible, they are dependent on others to do it for them.

When kids don't learn to think, process information, make decisions and be responsible, they are dependent on others to do it for them. This becomes a reality when, as young adults, these kids depend on the government, churches, charitable agencies and their families and friends to take care of them and get their stuff done, with them or for them.

Lessons Learned

Jake's teammate told him he was their best player and they needed him on the field. He could see they had the same size feet, so he told Jake he would share his shoes with him and they would take turns wearing them during the game.

On the way home from the game, Beth asked Jake if his teammate had been the one to forget his shoe, would he have loaned his shoe to him. Jake told his mom since he was the better player, he would not have. She then asked him how his teammate's generosity made him feel. Jake admitted it made him feel good. Beth asked Jake if he had taken the time to let his teammate know he was thankful he unselfishly shared his shoe with him.

Jake told his mom his teammate knew he was grateful for helping him. Beth asked him how his teammate knew Jake appreciated his generosity since all she saw was Jake grab the shoe and put it on as he was running out to the field. She asked him if he had loaned his shoe to a teammate for the same reason, would Jake want the teammate to show him he was grateful. Jake called this teammate when he got home to do just that.

The day before the next game, Jake went to his mother and told her all his gear was in his bag and it was by the door ready to go. Beth had been in the kitchen trying to decide whether she should remind him to get it done, so she was delighted to hear this and told him so. She asked him if he needed to be reminded in the future, and he told her she was off the hook and he was going to make sure all his gear was in the bag from now on.

The Helicopter Parent

When talking with Beth about Jake, I told her to stop hovering over him like a helicopter hovers over its target or landing pad. Wanting to protect their kids, parents watch for any pitfalls they could get caught in, and step in to smooth it out before their kids approach it.

What are you teaching your child when you smooth out their day so they don't run into any potholes? How else is your child going to learn how to handle the unexpected?

Your child doesn't want to become responsible, so you are going to have to train him to be, which means you need to be determined to outlast his stubborn intent to continue to do things his own way.

Teaching Responsibility

How do you teach your kids to be responsible? While this may seem an impossible ideal, in reality it can be done and will make your life and home peaceful. First of all, your child doesn't want to become responsible, so you are going to have to train him to be, which means you need to be determined to outlast his stubborn intent to continue to do things his own way.

Training your children to be responsible has three parts:

1. **Giving information** – Again, your child needs to know *what* he is supposed to do and *why* he is supposed to do it. This is a teaching time. My kids knew I (Carla) would start teaching times by looking up the definitions of words such as "responsibility" together and read verses from the Bible on this topic. I would work with the kids to come up with ways to put what we were discussing into practice.

   - When teaching on responsibility, when your child is told to get a job done like clean his room, ask him what he thinks he has to do to accomplish this. For the purposes of this illustration, we are talking about kids' ages 7-10 years. Go to his room and have him tell you what needs to be done for the room to look clean. You might be very surprised to find out what his idea of a clean room is and what your idea of a clean room is are as far apart as the east is from the west.

   - Once you both settle on what a clean room looks like, ask your child what he needs to do to get it clean and have him make a list. He can write down things like he will put his pajamas away where they go, put his cars and trucks in the bin on the shelf, pick up the things on the floor, and so forth. The more specific he is, the more likely he will take ownership of getting this task done correctly.

   - For children younger than seven years of age, find or draw pictures of all they need to do to clean their room and make them a picture chart that can be easily followed when you say, "Go clean your room."

2. **Show how it is done** - All too often parents only give information to their children. Kids also need a picture of what accomplishing this looks like. Go to his room and clean it together, making sure he understands exactly how you want the agreed upon cleaning done.

3. **Hold them accountable** – There is no point taking the time to give your kids information about something, show them how they are supposed to do it and then wave at them, wishing them good luck and turn your back on them and walk away. This is what it looks like to your kids when you are not willing to put in the effort to hold them accountable for what you have just shown them how to do. Whether it is cleaning a room or being kind to a sibling, holding your child accountable for how he handles this is key.

Does this work for teens too? Absolutely!

- When your teenager is not responsible in getting his chores done, pick one, like cleaning his room and ask him what he thinks you mean by this. Go to his messy room and ask him to tell you what needs to be done for the room to be clean to your standard. The tone of your voice needs to be calm and non-confrontational. Write down what he/she says. Then ask him to tell you what it means to be cleaned to his standard and write down what he says.

- If you are a perfectionist, please realize your kids don't have to be one too. To get a different adult perspective, ask your spouse what he/she thinks a teenager's bedroom needs to look like for it to be considered clean. When I (Carla) was trying to come up with a compromise when working with my teens, I would picture myself at a friend's house walking to the bathroom, passing their teen's room on the way. If I looked inside, what would my first impression of "clean" be? I realized if the room was picked up and the bed made, I would think it looked good. This helped me get perspective when working with my own teens.

Instead of giving my teens my perfectionistic standard of "clean", I worked with them to come up with a list of what "picked up" looked like. When my teens realized I was willing to lower my standard, they added things to their list and we were finally on the same page regarding getting their rooms clean.

This is a great way to teach your kids and teens what ***compromise*** is, a skill they will need to use their entire lives. You are building a trusting relationship between you and your kids when you are willing to compromise in an area that is not moral. The more you work with them through dialogue instead of confrontation, the more they will respect you and show a willingness to bring things they are concerned about to you in the future.

What Parents Can Do

When training your children to be responsible, make sure you and your spouse are on the same page and are working together. If you aren't, your children will pick up on this and pit you against one another.

You will need to be observant, watching your children to see how they are progressing when they are in the training phase of working on assuming ownership of a new behavior.

When training your children to be responsible, make sure you and your spouse are on the same page and are working together.

Watch for areas your child isn't following through on. Take him out for ice cream (a neutral place lets him know he isn't in trouble), and ask him why he isn't getting his stuff done. Ask him what he needs to do to become more **consistent** in following through with tasks. Ask him what you can do to help him with this. Hold him accountable for getting things done.

When holding your child accountable, you will need to find a way to remind yourself to remember to check and see if he has finished the task. For teens, ask them to come and let you know when they have completed the task, whether it is doing a chore or their schoolwork. Have a consequence ready you and your spouse agree upon for specific behaviors. When you know in advance what consequence you are going to give for a behavior, it is much easier to give it instead of a lecture when the time comes.

Be willing to have your child do the task over again if it was not done correctly. Kids need to learn to do a task right when it is given to them. Do not do a task for your child you have already given him to do. No one is going to follow him around when he is an adult and do his jobs for him.

Only give your child **one** behavior to take ownership of at a time. When he gets 75% consistent with it, work with him to take ownership of another area of his life.

It Isn't the Easy Way

Working with your kids to take ownership of their responsibilities, which requires them to think for themselves isn't easy. To do this, you have to think! We know you are busy with your own activities plus you chauffeur your kids to practices and games and music lessons and so on. All of this takes your time. Making it a priority to teach and train your children to be responsible is well worth the sacrifice however.

When your kids are in their mid-twenties, do you think they will look back and thank you for taking the time to get them to soccer practice or will they look to you with a grateful heart for teaching them to be responsible?

Our son and his wife took us out to lunch one day a few years ago. He had just gotten a promotion and a raise at work. He told us a lot of his job productivity where he was employed had as much to do with his work ethic as it did his talents and skill in his profession. Skills can be learned, but a work ethic? Taking on an employee with a poor work ethic is a can of worms no employer wants to open.

During lunch, our son thanked us for not giving up on him when he was growing up in our home. He said he knew he didn't make it easy on us, but he was grateful we had taken the time to teach him how to work.

"Teaching your kids to be responsible takes your time, energy and consistent effort. I (Denise) often am the one who wants to soften their way and be the "responsible" mom. I am thankful God gave me a husband who put our kids into positions where they had to think for themselves and solve their own problems whenever possible. As parents, we have found if we are not on the same page and are not working together as a team to train our children to be responsible, resentment towards each other builds up which the kids quickly pick up on. Even though we are opposites in so many ways, we come together as a couple knowing that part of being a family is showing our kids what a united marriage looks like.

Family identity has always been important to our family. The phrase, "Work Hard—Work Fast" has long been a family motto. As parents, we understood we needed to model a strong work ethic for our kids. Owning our own business gave us an environment to do this. This work ethic produced responsible children who grew into responsible young adults. We trained our children since early childhood to take ownership of their chores and schoolwork. We wanted them to not only complete their duties but to do a quality job as well.

Our two sons are now young men who work hard at their jobs, caring as much about their integrity as they do their work. Our daughter is in high school, and she consistently shows others how to have fun while they put their best effort into whatever they are doing. As our kids have grown and a daughter-in-law has been added into the mix, we are still a tight family who likes to work and play together. We thank God for this every day.

Joey Link was our youth pastor when we were teens. In fact, he led Joe to salvation through Jesus Christ. When our first child came along, Carla and Joey were visiting friends and family in Southern California and came to our church one Sunday. I left the service and Carla followed me out, finding me in the bathroom crying right along with our three-week-old son. She took time out of their vacation to help me get my life back in order. We are grateful they have been our parenting mentors all these years. They always encourage us to keep God first in our lives, our marriage and our parenting. The information you are reading in this book is the information they shared with us as our children were growing up. We pray you will put it into practice so you will see the fruit of this great teaching."

-Joe and Denise, California

"Whatever you do, work heartily as for the Lord and not for men, knowing that from the Lord you will receive the inheritance as your reward.
You are serving the Lord Christ. "
Colossians 3:23-24

Chapter 4

How Parents Stop Kids
from Thinking

We were visiting with a friend who worked as the director of student services at a large university. As we chatted with him about this book, he told us he was glad we chose this topic to write on as they dealt with "way too many" kids who didn't know how to think for themselves and could not function on their own at school.

He asked us to give him a synopsis of why we think this is such a big problem. I (Joey) told him the reason intelligent kids get to college and are not able to manage their time in order to get to classes on time, get their papers turned in or make time to study for exams without burning themselves out, much less hold a part-time job is because they have never done so for themselves until they moved to the college campus.

They haven't had to, because their parents have managed their time for them, including getting them out of bed in the morning, keeping track of homework assignments for them and so on until they left their home to go to college. Society has come up with a word for this phenomenon and it is "entitlement". Kids who don't have to think about how to manage their time, get their responsibilities completed and have the freedom to do whatever makes them happy think they are owed whatever they want and they don't think they have to work for anything. When they move into a dorm room with roommates, their awakening is rude indeed.

Parents Stop Their Kids from Thinking

Let's look at the ways parents stop their kids from thinking, unintentionally for the most part. As much as I wondered why my kids would not think for themselves, it never occurred to me (Carla) I was doing their thinking for them.

Parents who don't expect their kids to succeed have kids who don't.

How do parents stop their kids from thinking for themselves? The following are some of the most common ways:

1. **Reminders, reminders, reminders**–When you remind your kids, you are doing their thinking for them. You are teaching your kids they don't have to listen because you will tell them again and again what they need to do, and they only have to pay attention when your tone of voice and body language lets them know they need to wave the white flag in surrender and they better snap to it.

2. **Lectures** – Unless you have new information to give your child, stop lecturing. What do you do instead? We will get to that later.

3. **Anger** – When parents get angry, they yell at their kids, often not caring what they say. Angry parents do not raise kids who think for themselves. They raise kids who will do whatever it takes to calm their parents down or get away from them.

4. **Busyness** – Busy parents don't have time to wait their kids out to see if they are going to work it out for them-selves. It is easier to tell their kids what to do and pray they get it done.

5. **Expectations** – Parents who don't expect their kids to succeed have kids who don't. If you expect your child to pick up his backpack, he will. How does your child know you expect him to? Kids know what their parents' expectations are when they refuse to bail them out on a regular basis and they give them consequences when they don't follow through with their responsibilities.

6. **Well-trained** – Parents are supposed to teach and train their kids, but often it is the other way around. Kids train their parents. Jake trained his mom to run home and get whatever he left behind, and it wasn't only for his soccer shoes. He regularly forgot to get his homework in his backpack before he left for school and get his chores done too. He didn't have to think because when he "forgot", Beth jumped into action. She was his back-up plan.

Kids Have Invisible Power

Kids have overwhelming power over their parents. It's called *embarrassment*. Every parent wants to be proud of their kids and they want them to succeed in life. They also want them to look good in front of others. They don't want Grandma to see messy bedrooms when she visits, so mom cleans them. Parents want their kids to make the honor roll so they make sure they get their schoolwork turned in on time.

We have friends whose teens had a habit of missing the bus because they weren't ready for school on time. As the school was over thirty minutes away, Mom had to hustle to get everyone there before the bell rang. I (Carla) asked her why she was taking them to school when they missed the bus. What was the worst thing that would happen to her kids if they were late or if she didn't take them to school at all and they got an unexcused absence.

She told me if they were late three times, they would get detention. I asked her if she and her husband were willing to let them serve detention. She had to think about it a minute, then decided she was. She would check with her husband to make sure he was too.

Mom called again a few days later. The kids who were ready caught the bus. The ones who weren't asked her to take them to school. She told them it wasn't her responsibility to get them to school because they were messing around and weren't ready on time.

Her teens panicked, and as time dragged on they told their mom they would be late and would get a tardy. Mom just nodded her head and suggested they come up with a way to take ownership of getting to the bus on time. The teens ended up reimbursing their mom for the gas in the car and for the time it took her to get to school and back. After this experience they made it a habit to get to the bus stop on time in the morning.

All too often, parents bail their kids out by hovering over them, reminding them, lecturing them and turning into downright nags. Because it is important to parents their kids look good in front of others, they do this to save their own reputation as well as pave the way for their kids to avoid the consequences of their irresponsible choices. Once our friends decided if their teens earned detention they would serve it, how to deal with their inability to get ready on time became crystal clear.

Wrong Choices

Notice above where we said parents pave the way for their kids to avoid the consequences of their irresponsible choices. Kids choose to forget, they choose not to remember, and they choose to avoid doing their chores and other responsibilities.

> *Kids choose to forget, they choose not to remember, and they choose to avoid doing their chores and other responsibilities*

What makes parents lecture their kids? It is not forgetfulness. It is not a faulty memory. It is the choices their kids are making which gives them too many freedoms. Kids know exactly what they need to do, but they choose not to do it.

Jake was not characterized by choosing to remember to make his bed, pick up his clothes, feed the dog or get his homework done, even when reminded, so why would Beth expect him to choose to remember to get his soccer gear in the bag? The next time your child forgets, ask yourself how often this happens, and you will soon see if he is in the habit of choosing not to remember.

Kids Can Forget

Kids can have something big come up that distracts them, or they can be stressed or overtired. These are times they will forget things they normally would have taken care of with ease. If your child is not characterized by choosing to forget, then when he does, give him reminders. This is absolutely the right time to do so.

Parental Transitional Training

Parenting is the process of transitioning information to your kids so they can grow in knowledge and become responsible and mature. Once information is transferred to your child and you are satisfied your child knows how to apply it, you need to give him ownership of it.

Giving ownership of a behavioral issue to your kids is an ongoing training process. It is far better for the kids to fail at something when they live in your home so you can continue to work with them on it than when they are on their own.

> *Once information is transferred to their child and the parents are satisfied their child knows how to apply it, they need to give him ownership of it.*

If parents continue to wake their child up for school at fourteen years of age, when will this child learn he needs to go to bed at a certain time and get himself up at a certain time leaving enough time to get ready in the morning? If these parents don't begin this transitional training process soon they will be frustrated when he can't get up for classes when he is in college and flunks out of school. Over the years we have heard this story over and over again.

Transitioning is Key

"Transition" is the key thought here. Parents transition knowledge to their kids then hold them accountable for using it appropriately. Holding your kids accountable for the knowledge they have received is how you give ownership of it to them. How do you do this? Give your kids time to learn how to use this knowledge wisely, then when they don't, give them consequences to remind them making wise choices is the best way to grow.

Ultimate Goal

The ultimate goal is for parents to work with their kids, teaching them how to think for themselves, and once they know how, hold them accountable for doing so. Once you have taught them about a specific responsibility and have given them ownership of it, you have to let your children feel the pain of losing the blessing of that responsibility when they refuse to think through how to handle it. Otherwise, they will be training you to think for them.

We encourage you to take a few days and keep track of how often you and your spouse remind, repeat instructions to or lecture each of your kids (over the age of 5 years). Doing each of these things is a habit, and will take a bit of time for you to break. By keeping track for a few days, you will know what you are up against when you begin to train your kids to think for themselves.

While your kids are learning to do things differently, so are you, which is the other reason we encourage you to work on one thing at a time. We are giving you lots of things to work on in this book. Make a list and put them in order of priority. When your kids have taken ownership of the one thing you decide to start with 75% of the time, start working on the next thing on the list. Don't get discouraged.

How are you stopping your kids from thinking for themselves? What can you do to change this?

"Despite the fact that we homeschool, our son Ethan does not enjoy school to the extent that he would often whine, complain, and challenge me on why he needed to study certain things. In

those moments it was very tempting to try to reason with him (another way to say I lecture him) on the need to learn and to have a good attitude about it. In the past I was guilty of trying such tactics with him. However, I learned through the Mom's Notes series by Joey and Carla that there are more effective ways of helping kids choose to obey with a good attitude.

Whenever I recognized my son was having a bad attitude regarding school, I would have him sit on the stairs and think about his attitude and what he needed to do to change it. Some days Ethan sat on the stairs and thought for an hour or more. Other days he sat on the stairs and thought for only a few minutes. The length of time he sat was not important.

The important part was the lecturing. I was not lecturing my son as he sat on the stairs thinking. Ethan was lecturing himself. I was not telling my son he was being ungrateful, uncooperative, and disrespectful. Ethan was telling himself that his attitude was wrong and needed to be corrected. He was doing his own thinking. He was choosing to behave differently by talking himself into having a good attitude and getting his schoolwork done.

I recently asked Ethan, who is now fifteen years-old, if having him sit when he had a bad attitude was helpful. He replied that it was the only way he would have ever changed his attitude, because it allowed him to make the choice to change rather than being lectured or forced into it by me.

A few months ago we moved across the country (Marty is in the army). We are no strangers to moves, but literally moving halfway across the country is like moving to a new culture. This requires re-learning how to do normal things because everything is different here, and my husband and I started reminding our kids again. A few nights ago we sat down with Ethan and talked about this. He listed four areas we constantly reminded him in and shared how he is going to work on these things. Learning so long ago to ask questions instead of arguing and lecturing our kids taught our son how to think for himself. We are grateful for the young man he is maturing into, and for this teaching that helped get him there."

-Marty and Tricia, Washington

"For the Lord gives wisdom; from his mouth come knowledge and understanding."
Proverbs 2:6

Chapter 5

Why Kids Don't Think

Our son Michael bought a house a few years ago that needed a lot of work done to it. He and his wife worked night and day on it for a few weeks before they moved in to it. Having purchased two "fixer-uppers" ourselves, we could certainly appreciate the time, effort, and labor it took to get the repairs and renovations done. Even though they live several hours away, I (Joey) enjoyed getting to work with him on the house one long weekend.

Over the years, I have praised our son for the good work I could see he was doing on the house when we visited them. I often wondered where he had acquired the knowledge he needed to do the work on his house in specific areas. On a recent visit to our home, Michael and I were in a particular room of our house and he told me he learned how to do electrical work in this room.

To say I was surprised would be an understatement. I remember having him help me put outlets in the room when he was a teenager, but I don't remember teaching him about electrical work. When Michael told me he was watching and asked questions all those years ago, I was a proud Dad, glad I had passed this down to my son. He was thinking it through as we were working on that project and in the process he was learning how to do it himself.

Kids, including teenagers pick up on more than we think they do. They are observing and they are learning. As parents, let's remember to give them something worth learning as we go about daily living.

Emotional Thinking

Most of us have done things we wish we hadn't at a younger age. Being young and "too big for their britches", teens do what they want to do when they want to do it, thinking in the moment.

"Thinking" is defined as *"the process of using one's mind to consider or reason about something."* [1]

All too often, kids use their emotions when they act or react to something, not their minds.

"She won't share with me," 5 year-old Sissy yelled. "I don't like it when she won't share with me so I'm not going to share with her!"

"Henry wanted me to help him with his homework," 9 year-old Timmy said. "He didn't pick me to be on his team when we were playing ball during recess and it was embarrassing to be the last one picked, so I told him he wasn't getting any help from me."

"She cut me off!" 17 year-old Ashley hollered. "I will show her how it feels to be cut off!" as she sped the car up to pull in front of the lady.

There is nothing wrong with emotional thinking as long as the emotion in question is under control before a decision is made. The three children mentioned above do not have emotions that are under control. Their decisions are fueled by anger and need parental intervention.

We are sure if we took a survey, most adults would say they have made many subjective decisions (with their emotions) they wish they could take back because their perspective was skewed by what they were feeling at the time. Objective thinking produces decisions one can count on to stand firm in the face of rough terrain ahead.

Thinking Objectively

Subjective thinking often gets kids into trouble. Kids need to learn how to think with their minds to grow into maturity and become responsible adults. Parents need to help their kids

> *Objective thinking produces decisions one can count on to stand firm in the face of rough terrain ahead.*

learn to objectively reason or think through issues they face in their daily lives to make the smartest and wisest decisions.

If you are familiar with the four basic temperaments, a blend of which we are all born with, kids with the melancholy and sanguine temperaments have difficulty being objective as they are led by their emotions in how they approach life. We will talk more about temperaments in a later chapter.

Rational Thinking Defined

"Thinking" is also defined as, "*to employ one's mind rationally in evaluating or dealing with a given situation.*"[2]

In order to think for themselves, kids need to learn to rationally evaluate situations, circumstances and problems they face.

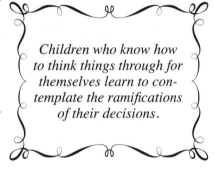

Children who know how to think things through for themselves learn to contemplate the ramifications of their decisions.

Children who know how to think things through for themselves learn to contemplate the ramifications of their decisions. They use their intelligence and logic to learn to process concepts and work through issues to make the best decision in a given circumstance. They seek advice and counsel from others when they are unsure what the wisest decision would be.

Non-thinking kids don't use rational judgment. They are looking for short-cuts and how they can please themselves in spite of how it will affect or impact themselves, their family members or their family's good name.

Why Kids Don't Think

No one wants irresponsible kids. Teaching your kids to be responsible will affect every area of their life every single day of their life. How are they going to live on their own and make it through college if they aren't responsible? What kind of employee or spouse are they going to be if they're not responsible, not to mention how they will raise your future grandchildren.

Kids know if they don't think:

1. **Their parents will tell them what to do.** We have already shared this but it is worth repeating. Kids are more than happy to let their parents make their decisions and tell them what they should be doing while the kids evaluate if they want to do what they are being told to do or not. They know if they don't, they most likely will only get a threat, a reminder, or perhaps a lecture from you.

2. **Their parents will make the final decision.** Kids are not invested in the decisions their parents make for them. Braeden is supposed to get a job for the summer but puts it off. Dad finally asks a friend to give his son a job. His friend agrees, but soon wishes he hadn't. Braeden, thinking the family friend won't fire him, shows up for work late, if at all, and distracts the other employees from getting their work done when he is there. He is never going to take ownership of a job he did not want in the first place.

3. **Their parents will allow their kids to have too many freedoms.** When kids have too many freedoms, too much money and not enough responsibility, they live from day to day without thinking about tomorrow. I (Joey) remember when our son was around thirteen years old and he wanted a new mountain bike. I could have bought it for him, but I wanted him to learn to work, so I had him think through how he could earn enough money to pay for it. He came up with a plan and when he got the bike he was proud that he had earned the money for it himself. It took him seven months, but it became a great life lesson for him.

4. **Their parents will keep the promises their kids make.** Kids make promises but don't think through what it will take to keep those promises so their parents bail them out. Our daughter Briana wanted a guinea pig. Aside from

Carla not being overly fond of animals, especially ones that lived in the house, we weren't sure Briana would be responsible enough to take care of one and we surely were not going to take care of it ourselves. She promised us she would always take care of it, but we still had doubts.

We decided she needed to count the cost of what it would take to be the caretaker of an animal. We had her read books and do a report showing the cost and what was involved in caring for this pet. After a month of her processing all this, she wrote a great report. When Carla and I read it, we looked at each other and said, "How do we say 'No'?!" She got the pet and Freckles the guinea pig lived in our home for many years, well-loved and well cared for by her mistress.

Taking the Time to Show Them How

What does teaching a child how to think look like? Our daughter Amy decided to attend a college located in another state to get the best education for her field of interest. For various reasons, it was decided she would live in an apartment on her own. Since she had never lived anywhere but in our home, this in itself was an entirely new experience for her.

She knew we were going to help her with finances if we could, but we were waiting to see how much she needed from us. Instead of stepping in and figuring it out for her, I (Joey) asked her to come up with a budget. She had trouble figuring out how much money she would need each month for food. Carla had her make a menu for a month's period of time. Amy wrote down all the ingredients she would need and she went shopping with her mom. They talked about buying generic products versus name brands, read labels and priced the items on her list.

When they got to the cleaning supplies aisle, Carla asked her if she would need any of these items, knowing she hadn't put them on her list. By the time they had written the cost down for everything on her revised list, Amy had a good idea of how much money to budget for groceries.

Getting Amy to work on a budget, which she stuck to throughout her college career, took a lot of my time, which I willingly gave to her. Carla spent many hours showing her how to put a monthly menu together and going shopping with her, which she enjoyed doing. Taking the time to show Amy how to budget her money, how to take care of a home and car and all the other things a child never thinks about until he is on his own was a lot of fun and worth the time.

Working It All Through

The 13 year-old daughter of friends of ours wanted to spend the weekend doing things with her friends. Her mom was tempted to remind Alyssa of the science project due on Monday. She and her husband were teaching Alyssa to think for herself, so her mom resisted the urge to remind her of the project and instead asked her what her plan was to complete it on time.

Alyssa shrugged and said she would get it done and asked if she could go to her friend's house and spend the night. Her mom told her she didn't have the freedom to go until she told her when she was going to get the project done. Alyssa thought about it for a minute and said she would work on it when she got home the next day.

Alyssa's mom asked her what time she would be going to bed at her friend's house. Alyssa told her mom they would stay up late and seeing where her mom was headed with this conversation, Alyssa admitted if she was over-tired she would sleep the next afternoon instead of doing the project. After thinking about it some more and realizing her family had many things on tap for the weekend, Alyssa decided to stay home and get the project done so she wouldn't have it hanging over her head all weekend.

When her friend complained to Alyssa, saying her mother was a tyrant for making her stay home and do schoolwork, Alyssa told her friend her mom had left that decision up to her. Being able to say this made Alyssa feel proud of her decision, and she applied herself to finishing the project throughout the weekend. Alyssa did get a good grade on the project and her mom told her she was proud of her for doing well, but she went on to say she was more than proud of Alyssa for making the hard choice to tell her friend she wouldn't be coming over to spend the night.

Instead of telling your children what they need to do, taking the time to work through with them what they need to do and teaching them to look at the big picture in the process is a habit most parents will need to develop. It is hard not to just give them the answers, but our children would all tell you now they are grateful we taught them to think things through and problem-solve for themselves. This alone helped them face adulthood with confidence in their decision-making ability.

The "P" Word

When kids are capable of using rational judgment but they don't, frustrated parents fall back on the good old stand-bys — reminders, threats, manipulation, guilt and lectures. Instead of getting kids to think rationally, this drives them to think with their emotions and anger usually erupts on the part of both the kids and their parents.

> *When kids are capable of using rational judgment but they don't, frustrated parents fall back on the good old stand-bys - reminders, threats, manipulation, guilt and lectures.*

When our son was a teenager, we could easily see his potential. However, he was not in the habit of applying himself because his bare minimum was better than a lot of his peers' best efforts. We knew he had to learn the value of putting forth more effort than to just get by. I (Joey) was having a talk with him one day, trying to find a way to motivate him to step it up a notch in the way he approached things like schoolwork.

I said, "Michael, you have so much potential which you're not applying. You're not thinking about how to be the best you can be in your life and for God."

I wanted him to think about why God created him and what God could do in and through his life, but he didn't want to hear it from me. Every few days in our conversations I kept going back to the "P" word – letting him know how much potential he had and how he needed to make wiser choices. After a few weeks, we did see he was making smarter choices and we made sure we encouraged him for it.

Today, I couldn't be prouder of the way he is using the "P" word in his life. He is definitely living up to his potential. In fact, one day we were driving down the road and he was telling me some good things that he was accomplishing at work. I was so impressed I asked him if he remembered those conversations when I told him he wasn't living up to his potential. With a smile, he said he most certainly did.

The son we are so proud of today because of how he is applying his potential is the same boy who could not remember to take the trash out to the curb on Monday nights when he was a teenager. We told him he needed to come up with a way to remember to do this weekly chore because we were tired of remembering it for him.

He tried several things that didn't work and it finally took the consequence of having to load the garbage can in his car and drive it to the dump to get him to remember on his own. Having a stinky smell in his car and having to drive to the dump on dirty, dusty roads was the only reminder he needed for a very long time.

We will admit there were times we shuddered to think what his adult years would look like. We couldn't be prouder of the man, husband, father, son and employee he is today.

Taking the time to show your kids how to learn to think things through for themselves often means parents give up things they want to do. Joey didn't always make it to the YMCA to work out or get a game of racquetball in and I gave up attending a Women's Bible Study group, but when your kids are grown you will have time for all these things and more.

When your kids are gone, you can't get them back. Don't look back with regret. Take the time now to train your children how to think and be responsible. You don't get a second chance at parenting.

Do you have kids who think with their emotions? The next two chapters will share how to work with them to teach them how to think objectively.

"During the years of raising our four boys, now teens and young adult men, we have learned the importance of asking questions to make them think on their own. When we began applying this principle during their middle years, it taught them to think responsibly. This helped us influence them towards Godly decisions rather than deal with their irresponsibility instead. As a mom and dad who have a tendency to practice authoritarian parenting methods, attempting to control our children's thoughts and decisions only led to frustration and resistance.

For example, as we worked with our boys regarding their choice of friends, we soon realized we could not choose their friends for them. We learned to ask them what kind of qualities they would want in a friend and allowed them to evaluate the characteristics of their potential friend on their own. This taught our boys to critically think about their friendships instead of emotionally reacting to us when we tried to choose friends for them. When we learned to ask our boys questions rather than lecture them, our home became a peaceful haven.

We had to learn that forcing our wisdom on them might solve the immediate circumstance, but we showed greater wisdom when we worked with them to learn how to develop wise decision making skills. Our part was to pose questions that they would not think of on their own because of their lack of life experience. As we allowed them the freedom to think and guide themselves to make moral and prudent decisions, they were able to develop this life trait they will each need to be successful."

-Darrell & Shaunette, Central Africa

*"If any of you lacks wisdom, let him ask God,
who gives generously to all without reproach,
and it will be given him."*
James 1:5

Chapter 6

The "Me, Myself and I" Syndrome

"Krista, your chores aren't done and it is almost time for dinner," Mom called from the kitchen. "Krista, get in here and tell me why you haven't done your chores yet. I don't want to hear excuses like you lost track of time working on the computer. You know your dad will have a fit if he comes home and your chores aren't done."

Let's review what we have learned so far in previous chapters. If you tell your kids they must do their chores, but when they don't get them done, you remind them, threaten them, yell at them, and they still don't do them, what are you teaching your kids?

Kids know why their parents are lecturing them before a word comes out of their parents' mouth. They probably can't count how many times they have heard the same lecture over and over again. In essence, you are teaching them they don't have to listen to "blah, blah, blah" and when you are done, they know you will remind them to get their tasks finished and bail them out when they don't. Kids learn these lessons well. Unfortunately, they don't understand why no one is reminding them what they need to do or following them around to make sure they get it done when they move out on their own.

If we as parents don't make our kids use their own mental energy to learn to think about what they need to do and how to get it done, how will they learn how to get into the habit of doing it? And when will they begin to think for themselves so you don't have to do all the thinking for them?

It's About Attitude

Our daughter Briana had missed forty plus days of school in both 2nd and 3rd grades because of chronic health issues. When the same cycle started the following year, her pediatrician encouraged us to home school her for several months to get her away from the germs other kids brought to the classroom.

The first few days she was at home for school Briana would tell me (Carla) she didn't feel good and needed to lie down. I soon learned she often did this at school and they would let her put her head on her desk or send her to the nurse's office to rest.

When I could get her to attempt to do school, her work was poorly done. It was obvious very little effort had gone into it. Briana's health problems were in her respiratory system. Being her mom, I knew when she was having trouble breathing and when she wasn't. It didn't take long for me to realize Briana just didn't want to do any schoolwork and she would tell me every day she was not breathing well enough to think straight. When I pushed her to get her schoolwork completed, her attitude would get uglier by the minute and her breathing as well.

One morning, I was done dealing with her attitude and I told her to go sit on her bed and stay there until she was willing to come to me and tell me she would not only submit to me as her teacher, she would do her work with a good attitude as well. She promptly retreated to her room with much wailing and alligator tears. In our home, when one of our children was told to sit to get their attitude straight, they were not allowed to do anything but sit.

Giving It Time

Briana would sit all day. When she did this, we sent her to bed immediately after dinner. She had lunch and dinner by herself after the rest of us had eaten. We had no idea how resilient and stubborn she could be.

Day after day I would ask her if she was going to submit to my instruction and off to her room she would go when she said "no." This went on for a few weeks and I knew she was getting way behind in school, but I had decided to be more stubborn than she was. Thankfully, the teacher who was overseeing her schooling was a like-minded friend and she assured me she would help Briana get back on track with her schoolwork once she got her attitude straight.

We attended a parenting conference out of state we were helping with and took the kids with us. I (Carla) was chatting with a group of women and Briana came up to me to ask me a question. One of the ladies asked Briana how she liked being home-schooled, and Briana told them she hadn't done any school yet.

Leaving the women staring after me, I swallowed my pride and escorted my daughter to the room she and her siblings were assigned to, pulled out a chair and told her to sit. Needless to say, she missed out on the fun activities our hosts had planned for our kids.

One morning not long after this, when I asked Briana if she was willing to submit to my instruction as her teacher, she told me she was. When I asked her if she was going to have a good attitude about doing her schoolwork, she responded she would, and she did.

It had been a difficult time waiting her out, but the dividends far outweighed the negative. The cheerful girl with the willing and teachable heart we got as a result was well worth waiting for.

Heart-Training

Heart training is definitely harder on the parents than it is on kids. There were many days Briana's father or I wanted to go in to her and wring her pretty little neck! Our hard-earned patience did pay off, and once Briana decided to do school with a good attitude, she caught up on all the work she had missed in half the time it would have taken her to do it in school. How was this possible?

As her teacher, I could have fought with her day in and day out to listen to my instruction and get her work done on time. If

I had chosen this path, she wouldn't have put appropriate effort into the work, getting less than satisfactory grades.

Parents get frustrated with their kids when they do their chores wearing their bad attitude all over their face. To top it off, all you end up with is a task or chore that has been poorly done while you listened to your kids whine and complain the entire time they were doing it. It doesn't have to be this way.

By telling her she would not do school until she was willing to look me in the eye and tell me she was going to submit to my instruction, I was working with Briana's heart. It really wasn't about getting the assigned work completed; it was about having a heart that was willing to learn with a good attitude. This is what we call "having a teachable heart." She quickly caught up on the work she had missed because her heart was in the right place so her attitude was too.

Teachable Hearts

If one's heart is not teachable, it is not willing to learn because it thinks it already knows everything it needs to know. When someone in authority, such as a parent, a teacher, coach, the law and government tries to tell this heart what to do, it rebels. When a heart rebels, it finds ways to let everyone know it is better than they are and it doesn't have to listen and obey. Sound like anyone you know?

Children who have teachable hearts listen to their parents when they are giving them direction or guidance.

What Makes a Child's Heart Teachable?

What makes a child's heart teachable and ready to learn? Here are some characteristics of children with teachable hearts.

1. **They are not focused on themselves.** The world encourages self-centeredness. Parents who give in to their child's whims and demands are training him to think the world revolves around him. The world as he knows it will not

always revolve around him, and the sooner he understands this, the better life will be. Teach your child to stop being "me-focused" and to start being "we-focused".

2. **They listen to their parents' direction.** Children who have teachable hearts listen to their parents when they are giving them direction or guidance. They ask questions when they don't know how or what to do. They trust their parents to give them good advice. They are characterized by obeying their parents and reap the blessings that come with their obedience.

> *"My son, be attentive to my words;*
> *incline your ear to my sayings...*
> *...keep them within your heart, for they are life*
> *to those who find them."*
> Proverbs 4:20-22

3. **They are humble.** Children who have teachable hearts are humble. They put pride and arrogance behind them. The definition of the word "humble" is *"the state of not thinking you are better than other people."* [2] It takes humility to listen and learn, because to be teachable, you have to be willing to admit there are things you do not know and you don't always do things the way they need to be done.

4. **They are characterized by making wise choices and decisions**. Children who have teachable hearts make choices based on what their parents have put into their hearts and on what the Bible says is true without anyone in authority telling them or reminding them to do so. This is how a child becomes morally mature and it is a process that takes years.

"A wise man's heart inclines him to the right,
but a fool's heart to the left.
Even when the fool walks on the road,
he lacks sense, and he says to everyone he is a fool."
Ecclesiastes 10:1, 2

5. **They admit when they are wrong and are willing to learn from their mistakes.** Children who have teachable hearts are willing to admit they are wrong without being forced to do so. Admitting they are wrong is just the first step. Next, they ask the one they offended for forgiveness and tell him how they are going to make the offense right. When our kids were younger they struggled with this process. We put together a family night to work through with them in a creative and memorable way how to remember the repentance, forgiveness and restoration process. (See Appendix A)

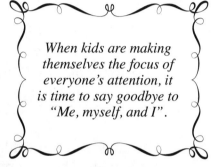

When kids are making themselves the focus of everyone's attention, it is time to say goodbye to "Me, myself, and I".

Me, Myself, and I

Kids think more of themselves than they think of others. Jesus turns this around when He tells us this in his second commandment:

"You shall love your neighbor as yourself."
Matthew 22:39

But self-focused kids rephrase it to:

"Others need to love me as much as I love myself."

This obviously contradicts what Jesus said in Matthew 7:12:

*"So whatever you wish that others would do to you,
do also to them."*

One of the ways to say goodbye to "me, myself, and I" is to find ways for your kids to love others. In our opinion, loving others starts with one's siblings. For little ones, to love a sibling could mean they would willingly share a toy. For older siblings, it could mean taking the time to play a game with younger siblings.[1] Training your children should always start at home.

Having a Heart that Thinks of Others First

How do parents get their kids to think of others (outside their own family) before themselves? Show them how they can look for ways to help others instead of expecting others to always be there for them. Opening doors for people, especially the elderly, mothers with young children and the disabled when your kids are in public is a place to start.

A family was going to the local mall. Their 8 year-old son, William was walking in front of his parents. As he reached the doors and was opening them to go in, an elderly couple was coming out at the same time. Instead of thinking about helping the couple,

Thinking hearts put the needs of others above their own.

William was only thinking about what he wanted to see when he got inside, so he rushed through the door and let it shut behind him. His dad grabbed the door and held it open for this couple to walk through. Dad called out to his son to slow down and rejoin the family, but didn't think to reprimand him for not holding the door open for the elderly folks.

Later that night, his parents did talk about this with each other, and on their way to church the following Sunday, they brought the subject up. Dad asked his son this question:

"You are going in the doors at church and you have your hands full. Mom asked you to carry the diaper bag and her Bible along with yours. If you reach out to open the door, everything will fall on the ground. You see Mr. Smith coming to the door. What do you think he should do?"

William immediately said Mr. Smith should open the door for him. His dad asked him why he though Mr. Smith should do so. William told his dad Mr. Smith would open the door because he could see William needed help. William's dad told him Mr. Smith had gotten a call telling him he needed to be somewhere right away, so he was in a hurry. He wasn't thinking about William's hands being full, he was thinking about what he needed to do and rushed through the door. The door shut before William could get through.

William wasn't happy about this and told his dad Mr. Smith should have held the door open for him anyway. It would only have taken a few seconds to do so. Dad reminded William of the elderly couple at the mall. He asked William what he thought this couple thought of his unwillingness to take a few seconds of his time and hold the door open for them. William hung his head as he told his Dad they probably didn't think much of him.

When the family got to church, William not only held the door open for his family, he asked his parents if he could stand there for a few minutes and hold it open for others too. This is a beautiful picture of heart-training at work.

The apostle Paul said it this way in Philippians 2:3-4:

> *"Do nothing from rivalry or conceit, but in humility*
> *count others more significant than yourselves.*
> *Let each of you look not only to his own interests,*
> *but also to the interests of others."*

"*Let each of you look not only to his own interests, but also to the interests of others.*" So not only is it a good thing to do, teaching your kids to think of others before they think of their own needs and wants is the right thing to do. Thinking hearts put the needs of others above their own.

Remember John F. Kennedy's great challenge in his inaugural speech when he became President of the United States?

> *"Ask not what your country can do for you,
> ask what you can do for your country."³*

Think of it this way:

> *"Don't ask what your family can do for you,
> ask what you can do for your family!"*

Now that's a family motto worth having!

"Having two teenagers, we can certainly attest to how important it is to understand whether or not your child has a heart that is teachable. As Joey and Carla said, it is a process that takes time. Recently one of our children greatly encouraged us when he showed a teachable heart by putting others first instead of himself but a few days later it was obvious his heart was not open to instruction from us. At these times, we remind ourselves of the information shared in this book which encourages us to stay consistent with these principles. We know the time will come when this child will, more often than not, be characterized by an open and teachable heart.

On more than one occasion, Joey and Carla have helped us realize the importance of having our kids work through this process so they grasp this is a life lesson, not something we do to make their lives miserable. There are times our plans were interrupted because we had a child that decided to put his self-centered heart at the top of our priority list that day. In this moment, our best parenting strategy was needed the most. This was not the time to just "let the issue slide".

The Links are right, implementing this teaching is harder on us than it is on the kids, and there have been times that we wanted to give up, but being consistent and patient does pay off! By working through these principles we gained confidence in knowing our kids will have a moral and humble heart when they are not around us. When we receive a compliment about our children from other

71

adults, we are so glad we took the time to invest in our children's hearts. You will feel the same way."

-Brian and Jolee, New York

*"Do nothing from selfish ambition or conceit,
but in humility count others more significant than yourselves.
Let each of you look not only to his own interests,
but also to the interests of others."*
Philippians 2:3-4

Chapter 7

Re-Training a Stubborn Heart

*L*esli was parked in my driveway and texted me, asking if I (Joey) was available to talk to her about her daughter. As the story unfolded, Lesli shared how frustrated she was with her daughter, Shayla. We met this family when Shayla was 12 years-old. She is now 14 years-old and her parents have been busy re-training bad habits of hers for the past couple years. Working on heart training, they have made progress, but Shayla still has a ways to go.

On this particular day, Lesli started the conversation by sharing how disrespectful Shayla was when she spoke to her and how unkind she was to her younger brother. This scenario had played itself out over and over again in their home. Shayla would change for the short term, and a few weeks later, she would return to her old ways, driving her parent's crazy.

From the Mind to the Heart

Parents think one of the reasons their teens make bad choices comes from peer pressure. It's not about peer pressure; it is about **where** your child's beliefs are located.

What stops a kid from accepting his parents' teaching and training and making changes for the long term comes to about eighteen inches. You think your kids are getting it together, and then the slide starts. Kids change what they think and believe when something or someone else comes along and challenges their thought process. Many times this someone is their own mind saying "It's been long enough. I'm tired of doing it their way. It's time to do it MY way!" The teaching you have been giving them never hikes the eighteen inches down from their head to their hearts.

Shayla has been evaluating everything based on the information in her head and not what her parents have been putting into her heart. Therefore, to her mom's dismay, everything she chose and decided to do was changeable based on what she thought was right in that moment of time. She was not working off a solid foundation. She used whatever she was thinking and feeling to base her choices on and this changed from circumstance to circumstance (another problem with emotional thinking), making her life unpredictable.

This is not uncommon in kids who have grown up in church or in Christian homes. Since they have heard how the Bible says they need to live their lives all their lives and have been taught a lot of what is biblically right and wrong, you would think they would make better choices. But in reality, all that good teaching became head knowledge, not heart knowledge.

Until the biblical teaching you give your kids is implanted into their hearts, they mimic your faith without taking ownership of it. At some point, every human being has to take ownership of their personal belief system.[1]

Shayla's parents have been trying to teach her what is right and what is wrong, but they were working with Shayla's unteachable heart. She was not and had not been buying into what they had been trying to teach her for a long time. They often hit the bulls-eye of her heart, but their teaching bounced off and never took hold. It was like they were working with a moving target.

How can her parents transfer their teaching into this kid's heart so it sticks? Lesli sent me that urgent S.O.S. text because Shayla had done something that shamed herself and her family.

Erasing the Shame

Shayla attends a Christian school. One of her teachers said she did not turn in an assignment two weeks prior. Shayla decided her teacher was wrong and began arguing with him. He told her he was not wrong and Shayla called him a liar.

Lesli could not believe what Shayla had done. She called her husband, Steve, and he got so angry they decided to get a neutral perspective, which was me.

I encouraged Lesli to pick up her daughter from school and to refuse to talk to her during the car ride home. Lesli was to take Shayla home and wait for her to offer an apology before engaging her in conversation. Psalms 66:18 says:

> *"If I had cherished iniquity (sin) in my heart,*
> *the Lord will not have listened."*

I told Lesli if God doesn't hear us when we are in sin, why should she talk to Shayla until she was ready to confess her sin to them?

> *"If we say we have no sin, we deceive ourselves*
> *and the truth is not in us. If we confess our sins,*
> *he is faithful and just to forgive us our sins*
> *and to cleanse us from all unrighteousness."*
> I John 1:8-9

As parents, we look for the good in our children which we should do. But, do you have as your underlying perspective the conviction your child is a sinner who needs salvation first and then parental heart training?

> *"For all have sinned and fall short of the glory of God."*
> Romans 3:23

"All" doesn't leave anyone out. It means every single human being, from birth, is a sinner. In general, parents know when their child does something wrong, is not telling the truth, or is irresponsible. However, while parents know their child is capable of wrong-doing, they don't want to believe their child did something he knew was wrong because parents want to think the best of their children.

Parents have difficulty accepting wrong-doing when they have worked with their child to do what is right in a given area and get defensive when they hear about the worst of their kids from the school or others in authority.

Redefining Sin

Parents bend over backwards to rescue their child from what they see as false accusations or misunderstandings. When you look at the standard of sin however, and compare it with right and wrong using the Bible as the foundation, you can't argue with it.

For instance, many marriages break up over infidelity because people intellectualize having an affair as something that just "happens". It wasn't some-thing they planned to do, so it isn't wrong. Affairs among Christians are becoming more and more normal and accepted in the church. When was the last time you heard someone talk about an affair as adultery, the sin God calls it?

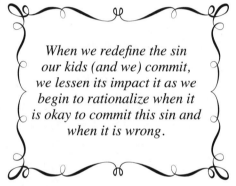

When we redefine the sin our kids (and we) commit, we lessen its impact it as we begin to rationalize when it is okay to commit this sin and when it is wrong.

Christians will say having an affair is wrong but will they say it is sin? If they admit it is sin, then they have to stop it or they won't be right with God. People rationalize it away because they say God wants them to be happy and if committing adultery makes them happy, there is nothing wrong with it.

Or, when was the last time you heard being intimate out of wedlock being called fornication or sexual immorality as the Bible does? When we redefine the sin our kids (and we) commit, we lessen its impact as we begin to rationalize when it is okay to commit this sin and when it is not.

When Lesli got to the school to pick up Shayla, she found her daughter had made the problem worse when talking to the principal. Using her honed debating skills, Shayla was trying to get him to agree she wasn't wrong for calling the teacher a liar. She wanted everyone to believe she did turn the assignment in, so the only explanation for its disappearance was the teacher must have lost it.

Shayla often forgot to turn assignments in on time, while the teacher was not characterized by losing assignments. Yet, she didn't get why people wouldn't believe her instead of him.

> *"...that your faith might not rest in the wisdom*
> *of men but in the power of God."*
> I Corinthians 2:5

The Ball is in the Parents' Court

Lesli didn't say a word all the way home from school. Knowing how much trouble she was in, Shayla tried to defend her actions to her mom like she did to the principal. Shayla was frustrated her mom did not respond to her, so when her mom told her to sit in a certain chair and not speak once they got home, Shayla didn't obey.

Instead, she followed her mom all over the house trying to get her to enter into a debate and negotiation with her, which was something she had successfully done many times before, causing major issues between her parents.

Meanwhile, Steve left work early so he and Lesli could work together to deal with their daughter. Steve called me on his way home and I told him this showed they had not been getting to Shayla's heart for some time, as she was doing what had worked for her before. Her dad was a born debater, and would, without thinking debate with Shayla when she started negotiating with him, thus elevating her to a peer level with him.

The time had come when Steve and Lesli were fed up with Shayla's rebellion and were willing to do whatever it took to turn her around because if she didn't humble herself and admit she was wrong for calling her teacher a liar, she would be kicked out of this school and they were running out of options to school her. Lesli didn't think she could home school Shayla for she was certain one of them would not survive a week.

When Steve got home, Shayla was finally sitting where her mom had told her to when they first got home. I asked them why Shayla sat in the chair when she learned her dad was on his way home. They realized she was somewhat intimidated by her dad, but obviously was not afraid of her mom.

They decided Shayla was not going to be joining family activities including meals, watching television or anything fun until she was willing to confess her sin, call it sin, apologize to those involved and share how she was going to earn the trust of her teacher and her family back after doing such a shameful thing. Kids need to know their sin not only embarrasses themselves, but their family as well.

Consequences Kick In

Later that evening as Lesli, Steve and their other children enjoyed dinner together, they talked and laughed, making fun plans for the weekend, knowing Shayla could hear them from the other room.

Before Shayla's bedtime, they could see she still had a hard look in her eyes, telling them her stubborn heart was not yet willing to repent and admit she had done anything wrong. Shayla was surprised when her dad told her she would be getting up at 5 a.m. and going to work with him because her hard heart had lost her the freedom of returning to school.

Shayla said nothing on the drive to work. Her dad put her in a room where she would not be bothered so she could think without distractions. A few hours later, her dad could see a softer heart and began the heart re-training process.

Re-Training a Stubborn Heart

Steve gave his daughter a piece of paper with 6 columns on it. (See Appendix B) He knew if he tried to talk to her they would fight and argue, so he decided keeping this discussion non-verbal was the way to go.

"What" sins did she commit was written at the top of the first column. Coming up with the sins she committed took Shayla a couple of hours. Knowing what you did wrong and admitting it

are two very different things. Her dad was going to let her take as much time as she needed to work on this because he knew she was battling what her heart was telling her.

At first, she put down one sin and the one she listed was accusing her teacher of lying. This did not surprise her dad since this was what everyone knew she had done. He gave her the paper back and told her there were a lot more sins she needed to write down.

When he went back into the room to see what else she had come up with a couple hours later, Shayla had written down she had not been obedient to her mother, she had been disrespectful to her teacher, she had been disrespectful to the principal by trying to get him to agree with her and she had stolen the night from her family since she would not admit to her sin.

Who Did She Sin Against?

Knowing these sins had been hard for his proud daughter to admit to, Steve decided to move on to the second column; *"Who"* she committed these sins against.

Shayla made her list and she came up with her Dad, Mom, brother, foster sister, teacher and principal in the *"Who"* column. Her dad told her there were others who were impacted by her sin too, and gave her back the list.

She added other names to this list, including those she had bragged to about what she had done. When her dad saw these names, he had her go back to the first column and write what sins she had committed against them.

How Does Sin Affect People

Dad wrote the word *"How"* at the top of the third column. How did Shayla's sin affect these people and/or impact them? Shayla worked on this for an hour and her dad came in again to see how she was doing. Dad was very pleased at the progress his daughter was making. He could see that Shayla was taking a serious look at herself, but he knew she had not yet gone deep enough.

He asked her who else was impacted by her sin and how they were affected by it. It took her a while, but Shayla finally realized all the teachers at the school most likely knew what she had done and she knew they would be thinking about it when she encountered them, especially the teachers of the other classes she was in.

Why and How

It was time to get to Shayla's heart. Too many times parents only deal with a partial list of their kids sins. This leaves many wrongs their child thinks can be negotiated at a later time. What happens when kids rationalize a sin and it bleeds into other areas in their heart?

These areas become compromised "just this once" which moves to "twice" and so on and it is not long before the teaching Mom and Dad have put into their hearts unravels and no longer looks like the Godly character the Bible says we should live by.

Shayla's dad was determined to get to the bottom of his daughter's heart, knowing that calling her teacher a liar was a symptom of a much bigger problem. He put the word "*Why*" at the top of the fourth column.

Shayla put down why she thought it was okay to tell her teacher he was a liar. She confessed she was prideful and she thought her teacher would believe she had turned the assignment in so he would think he must have misplaced it. Her dad sadly realized she thought her parents would believe the lies she told them as well.

Steve kept asking her questions he did not know the answer to, but he wanted to make sure Shayla scraped all the muck out of her hard heart. As a result, she came up with twelve more things she listed in this column.

She remembered doing the assignment, but she could not remember if she turned it in or not. She said her pride would not let her back down and her stubbornness wouldn't let her yield when her mom told her to sit in the chair when she got home. She admitted to being angry her mother would not listen to her even though Shayla wasn't planning on telling the truth.

She had to write down why she thought it was okay to have all these sin patterns firmly implanted in her heart. She had to really think about this and it took quite a while before she finished working on this list. When her dad came back in to see what she had come up with, he realized the sin patterns she listed had been building up in her heart for a very long time.

Why did Shayla work on these lists instead of sitting there continuing to pout? She could see the resolve in her parents and knew when her dad took her to work with him they were not going to back down. She realized her parents would keep her in "solitary confinement" until she gave in, and she did love her family and wanted to spend time with them.

Making Right the Wrong

"How" was the word at the top of the fifth column. How will she make these wrongs right? This is how relationships are restored and trust is rebuilt. In Alcoholics Anonymous 12-step program, alcoholics who work on completing the program must go back and make amends with the ones whose lives have been broken by their drinking. [2]

It is rare however, for parents to make their children go back and make things right with those they offend. The embarrassment of going to people and apologizing can teach a lesson that stays in kids' minds a long time. Going back and apologizing to people, especially peers, is difficult and humbling.

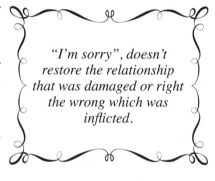

"I'm sorry", doesn't restore the relationship that was damaged or right the wrong which was inflicted.

Parents let their kids get off with "I'm sorry". All kids are sorry for is they got caught in their sin. "I'm sorry", doesn't restore the relationship that was damaged or right the wrong which was inflicted. Asking for forgiveness restores the relationship.

When our kids were young, after they said they were sorry and asked for forgiveness, we asked them what they were going to do to make it right. "Making it right" means the offender gives back what he took away with his sin. If he was unwilling to share his toys, he cheerfully offered to do so. If he didn't get his chores done, he told his parents he would do them as soon as he got home from school before he did anything else.

As they got older, we no longer asked our kids how they were going to make right their wrong. They knew to offer it when they were apologizing. Their apologies looked like this:

"Mom, I'm sorry I lied to you at church about where I was going. It was wrong because you need to know where I am and because God honors truthfulness. Will you forgive me? To make it right I will go to those who you were talking with at the time and tell them I lied to you and seek their forgiveness for doing so and the next time you ask me where I am going I will gladly let you know." (See Appendix A)

What Will Change?

There is one more column on the paper Shayla was working on. This one is the deal-breaker. *"What"* will make Shayla change this behavior so she won't do it again? When kids come up with ways to stand firm and not give in to this sin, they have an alternative when they are tempted to do it again.

What Shayla wrote down in this column showed her parents if she was humble or not. To be willing to change requires a humble, teachable heart. If they could see this in her responses to this question, although she had a long way to go, Shayla's parents could begin to open the door of trust again and it gave them a way to hold her accountable in the future when she lied again.

I suggested they take her out to dinner a few days later and review what she had written down on the chart. I told them to watch her body language and if she stayed relaxed and calm as they went through the lists, then her heart was in the right place. If she tensed up or refused to make eye contact with them, then they would know they had barely scratched the surface and she needed more time in isolation to think about her defiant, sinful ways.

Cleaning Up Her Reputation

I (Joey) have taught chapel at the Christian school Shayla goes to many times over the years and the principal of the school and I have become good friends. I ran into him one day while I was doing errands. Knowing I was working with this family, he told me about the apology he had received from Shayla for her attempt to draw him in to her sin by trying to get him to agree she was right and her teacher was indeed a liar.

It was a "Wow" moment for him. He had voluntarily received very few apologies over the years from kids who had done far worse things than Shayla had. He was very impressed with Shayla and her parents. When a child does what he said he would do to make his offense right, it gives him (or in this case her) back his reputation.

Shayla's teacher had been unwilling to have her in his class anymore. When she apologized to him and asked for his forgiveness, he gave it to her but he was determined Shayla would have to earn his trust back. What he found when Shayla came back to class was a student who was eager to make up the work she had missed. She asked questions when she didn't understand the assignment and she turned it in on time. Shayla was teachable and no longer challenged him.

Shayla's parents saw a different girl in their home as well. She wanted to be with the family instead of locking herself in her room. She asked her parents' questions and listened to their answers. They enjoyed seeing her begin to engage more with them on a deeper level and take their advice seriously.

Don't Get Too Comfortable

Did Shayla still have character issues that needed work? Absolutely! She had been defiant for a long, long time and this was just the start. She has a teachable heart now, and it makes all the difference for her parents. They know they have many issues still to conquer, but they know they will only see lasting results when they work on *one* of them at a time.

As I (Carla) am writing this, I thought, "This took a lot of time." We believe the number one reason parents are continually frustrated with their kids is they don't want to give up the time it takes to train them. We know you are busy. But once again, in fifteen years will you remember what you were busy with or will you be frustrated you don't have a relationship with your now adult children? Think about it.

Test Them

Did Shayla ever lie again? She did, just as you and I might do when we are backed into a corner and don't want to admit the truth. Should her parents have her work on these six columns every time they catch her? What do you think?

It all depends on Shayla's attitude. If she admits her wrong quickly then perhaps she didn't need to. But if her heart was hard and proud once again, then going through the process of answering all six questions might be what is needed to make her heart teachable.

> *When a heart is determined to have its own way, it can take a while until it is ready to see that God's way is better.*

When your child has gone through the repentance, forgiveness and restoration process successfully, parents need to look for an opportunity to test this child's heart by allowing him to be in situations where he is tempted to do wrong without reminding him to do right. If the repentance, forgiveness and restoration process was genuine on the child's part, the parent should get the appropriate response from him.

If you find your child's heart is not teachable, he gets to go sit again until he is ready to apologize with a truly humble heart. Don't get discouraged if your child has to go back and sit again and again, as Shayla did many times when she was working on the first two columns.

When a heart is determined to have its own way, it can take a while until it is ready to see that God's way is better. Keep isolating your child so he has time to think at a deeper level to work through the issues he doesn't want to deal with.

"Examine yourselves to see whether you are in the faith. Test yourselves. Or do you not realize this about yourselves that Jesus Chris is in you? Unless, indeed, you fail to meet the test. I hope you will find out that we have not failed the test."
2 Corinthians 13:5-6

What's Next?

In the next chapter we are going to share what you can do instead of giving into reminding and lecturing your child. Are you ready?

"Joey was the guest speaker for Chapel for the Christian school our kids attend. I (Lesli) got to talking with him and to say in the least he intrigued me. I went over to the Link's home that afternoon and spent a few hours talking parenting. Joey began meeting with us on a regular basis, taking us through the information in the parenting class he leads. Our children were 12 and 10 years of age at the time, and we needed help with our daughter.

Over the past two years we have determined that success in dealing with your children comes down to our resolve. The children will default back to unacceptable attitudes and behaviors very quickly if our resolve slips.

We were able to apply in-depth questioning to our daughter after a particular event. Her behavior was not tolerable nor acceptable to us or God. Had we only addressed her behavior we would have only resolved the issue at hand, but would not have reached the root of the problem. Following Joey's advice on how to use in-depth questions equipped us to perform "heart surgery" on our daughter. We were able to help her gain insight on how her actions affect others. More importantly, it allowed her to see how her head knowledge isn't transmitted through her actions because she is ruled by a sinful heart.

Heart-training is a slow and sometimes painful process because sin runs deep. Her desire to manipulate and justify are root issues that, through our faith, patience, resolve, and the guidance of the Links are being brought into the light so they can be destroyed.

Don't get discouraged if you have older children and have never before used teaching like what you are reading in this book. Don't get overwhelmed either. Take it one step at a time and you will see progress. Be more determined than your children are and you will succeed."

-Steve and Lesli, Iowa

""If I had cherished iniquity in my heart, the Lord would not have listened. But truly God has listened; he has attended to the voice of my prayer. Blessed be God, because he has not rejected my prayer or removed his steadfast love from me."
Psalm 66:18-20

Chapter 8

The Art of Asking Questions

*B*efore we had kids, we heard people tell horror stories about their children. Kids didn't do what they were supposed to do. They didn't do what they said they would do. They didn't keep their room clean, feed the dog, do their homework, practice the piano, or get along with their parents or siblings. When they did do something, they did such a poor job their parents had to fight with them to get them to do it over again.

Let's look at the other side of this coin. Being in youth ministry, this is what we heard from the pre-teens to the young adults we worked with.

"My parents won't listen to me, they just shout at me all the time."

"My parents just don't get it. I don't have any friends, Christians are walking freak shows."

"My room is clean enough. Trying to keep up with my Mom's idea of perfect is killing me."

"I'm a good kid but my parents keep me on such a tight leash they're choking me to death. I don't know what I have to do to get them to trust me. I'm not going to do anything stupid."

You would think these kinds of stories plus personal experience with the children of siblings and friends would stop people from having kids of their own, but for whatever reason, we all think it is going to be different with our own children. Why we think this, we are not sure, but we do.

You can count us in for making this mistake. I (Joey) was a youth pastor before going into family ministry and Carla's degree is in social work. We considered ourselves well prepared for the role of parents. We saw the mistakes others made from both sides of the coin and we were confident we would do better. Pride, as they say, goes before the fall, and our fall was a long way down.

We're Back to Lecturing

When parents don't know what else to do with their kids, or what they have been doing isn't working, they lecture. When parents lecture, they are trying to talk their kids into doing the right thing one more time. They don't understand why their kids just don't get it.

Kids "get it" all right; you just haven't talked them into doing anything, especially something they don't want to do. Parents are the ones who don't "get it".

Trying to talk kids into doing the right thing doesn't work because your words aren't going to motivate them to change. Lectures aren't consequences. They are just words, and they aren't words your kids haven't already heard many, many times before.

> *Lectures aren't consequences. They are just words, and they aren't words your kids haven't already heard many, many times before.*

So how do parents turn this around and get their kids moving down the right track? We are going to get to that, but first, we need to talk to you, the parent.

Problem = Parents

The responses you get when you ask questions will reveal the worst in your children. We know, you don't want to see the worst in your children. Who does? We want you to see the best in your kids and praise them for it, but you need to be willing to see and accept both sides of this coin. Again, as we talked about in the last chapter, when you are willing to see the worst in your children, you need to define it as ***sin***.

When parents see wrongdoing in their kids, it is easy to remind and lecture them and leave it at that. If parents see it as sin, it has to be dealt with for your children to have pure and cleansed hearts before God. When you continue to lecture your kids, you dig the unconfessed sin down deeper into their hearts so their behavior will get more difficult. Think of your questions as being the spade you dig these unhealthy roots out with!

There is a big difference between forgetting and choosing to forget.

> *"So whoever knows the right thing to do and fails to do it, for him it is sin."*
> James 4:17

While parents say they see the worst in their kids, in reality, they don't act like they do. When a child tells his mother he "forgot" to do something for the fourth or fifth time in a day, Mom still wants to believe her child really did forget once again, instead of realizing he is using "I forgot" as an excuse for not doing what he was supposed to do. There is a big difference between forgetting and choosing to forget.

When a teen wants to go to an event with his friends, parents don't want to deprive him of the fun of the event, so they lecture their teen instead of giving him a consequence for not getting his schoolwork done. Plus, when the teen promises his parents he will do better next time, they believe him.

Why do we believe our teens when they haven't been characterized by keeping their word or promises? Again, it's because we want to believe the best of them.

Kids Have It Figured Out

Our son would be as ornery as he could be and would kick it in gear and clean up his act if he wanted to go somewhere and do something fun, then he was back to being ornery and stubborn as soon as the event was over. We knew he was manipulating us but we just couldn't seem to get a handle on dealing with him.

When he was in high school, a popular Christian band was coming to town. They were going to have a concert in an open corn field on the outskirts of town. For a relatively small community in the Midwest, this was a rare happening and a huge event. Michael couldn't wait to go. This time however, he didn't pull his act together and he had been giving me 'what for' for a few weeks.

Joey and I were talking about this dilemma for the umpteenth time. I told him Michael shouldn't have the freedom to go to the concert. Joey disagreed with me. He said he just wasn't willing to take the concert away from him because it was a one-time event.

I was not happy, but waited to see if Michael's behavior improved. On a particularly bad afternoon, one of Michael's sisters told him if he didn't pull his act together we would take the concert away. He laughed and said his dad would never do that because he wanted him to go. How right Michael was.

At least we now knew why he hadn't been obeying us. He didn't have to because he knew his dad would let him go no matter what. On our weekly date, I asked Joey if a parent from church came to him and described their son in the same way we had been talking about Michael that evening, what advice would he give them.

Without skipping a beat he said he would tell them to take away their son's freedoms until he showed them respect once again. I asked him if going to the concert was a freedom. Joey realized he needed to set his own emotions aside and forbid Michael to go.

Parents need to recognize when it is time to take a step back and take their blinders off so they can see things from an objective perspective. If you or your spouse can't be objective, ask someone else you respect for their opinion. If you are a single parent, ask your parents or older friends for their thoughts. There is always someone to ask.

Taking the Blinders Off

Parents like the strengths in their kids, but don't like to be confronted with or deal with their weaknesses. When our kids were growing up, we would pray and ask God to remove our blinders where our kids' weaknesses were concerned and help us see the areas we needed to work on.

Don't pray this however, unless you are sure you are prepared to see the worst in your children, because when the blinders come off, you can no longer excuse away their sins you are trampling on every day.

We trusted teachers and other authorities in their lives to share with us what their weaknesses were as well. When our kids went to public school, we told them whatever the teacher said about them we would believe because the teacher had no reason to lie. I (Carla) remember going to our daughter Amy's first parent-teacher conference when she was in Kindergarten.

Amy is full of love and laughter and can talk your ear off. I had worked with her the year before she started public school to teach her how to sit, be patient when she colored and to listen without talking. However, I knew when she was in a classroom full of kids she would lose her focus and forget to do the things we had worked on because she was enjoying being surrounded by friends. I was prepared to hear the worst.

I asked the teacher what her issues with Amy were, and what suggestions she had for us to work on these things. The teacher about fell off the chair! She told me Amy was one of the best students in the class. Amy listened to the teacher and obeyed her instructions. She encouraged other kids to watch Amy and obey as well as she did. I was prepared to hear the worst of our daughter and was pleasantly surprised to hear the best instead.

Accept Their Weaknesses

We all come into this world with both strengths and weaknesses, so if we want one, we are going to have to accept the other! Instead of getting frustrated their weaknesses don't go away or get better, plan to proactively teach your children how to turn a weakness into strength. We encourage parents to take

91

the time and energy to come up with a plan to do this. You are giving them a skill for life.

I (Carla) remember the time our son, who was in his final year of high school, was pacing in our home office, muttering something I was sure was unkind about one of his sisters. When I asked him what was wrong, he listed her weaknesses without taking a breath.

I looked at him and said, "When I get angry with your father and start thinking of all his weaknesses to fuel my anger, I tell myself that in his mind, I have as many weaknesses as I think he does and if I don't want him to work on changing me, I can't work on changing him. You will be getting married in a few years and God gave you sisters to practice on. Try to re-focus your energy on the good things they do."

> *Accepting the weaknesses and imperfections in your children and teens will strengthen the bonds of respect and trust between you.*

It is hard to accept weakness in the ones we love, especially if you are a born "fixer", meaning when you see a problem you instinctively want to fix it. Accepting the weaknesses and imperfections in your children and teens will strengthen the bonds of respect and trust between you. It is well worth the self-discipline it might take.

It's in the Question

Lectures aren't discussions. They are one-sided conversations. Parents do all the talking and they think their kids are doing all the listening. In reality, nobody is listening. Anything your child tries to contribute during a lecture just makes you angrier. By the time parents get around to lecturing their kids, they are generally frustrated, angry and defensive. So, when you tell your child to close his mouth and listen to you, he turns both his mouth and his ears off.

Asking your kids questions instead of telling them what to do opens the door for a two-way conversation to take place. When parents ask the right questions, they will find out what their kids are really thinking which helps parents get needed perspective to get down to the root problem.

Lectures are based on what parents assume their kids are thinking. Asking questions allows parents to discover areas their children need additional training in so they can work with them to make wise choices the next time the same situation arises.

When to Ask Questions

Knowing **when** to ask questions and **what** questions to ask tends to stump even the most intelligent parent. The following are times when parents should ask their kids questions instead of lecturing them to get to the heart of what is going on.

When your child:

- Has done something wrong but doesn't want to admit it
- Has lied to you or someone else and he doesn't want to admit it
- Tries to steer you off-track by deceiving you
- Has not followed through on a task or responsibility as he knows he should, yet goes on to enjoy something he wants to do

What Questions to Ask

The questions parents ask their kids need to challenge the premise or foundation of their thinking. Parents should not accept answers that don't make sense or are not in line with Godly principles. The following are types of questions parents can ask their children when they are trying to get to the bottom of a situation.

- ✓ Why did you do that?
- ✓ What were you thinking when you decided to do that?
- ✓ Why didn't you do what I asked you to do?
- ✓ Did you feel guilty for not doing what I asked you to do? (By asking this you will see if their conscience is hardened)

✓ How do you think I felt when I found out you didn't do it? (Kids rarely think about their parent's feelings, so this teaches them compassion)

✓ Did you think you would get away with it? (This will show you if you are consistent with consequences)

✓ Did you think what you did was the right thing to do? If so, why?

✓ If not, what do you need to do about it now? (Make it right with ones he offended)

✓ What can you do instead the next time you are tempted in the same way?

✓ How will you make yourself do what is right when you don't want to?

✓ How are you going to regain our trust?

When you read through this list of questions, what kind of tone or voice did you read them with? I am guessing you read them with a calm tone. When you are frustrated or angry with one of your children, it would be easy to rattle off these types of questions in an angry tone which could sound like a lecture, especially if you were shooting them at your child like bullets from an automatic weapon without waiting for his response.

Be sure you have settled down before you start asking questions so you ask them in a way that won't shut your child down. And be sure to ask *one* question at a time and *wait* for a response. If your child is defiant or defensive in his responses to your questions, have him sit in an isolated spot until he calms down and then try again.

They Do Know

Kids will try to wiggle their way out of questions they don't want to answer. When you first start asking your kids questions instead of lecturing them, the most common response you will get is "I don't know."

To "not know" will be the exception, not the rule. Don't let your child or teen walk away after saying "I don't know." Tell your child to sit without talking (you choose where) until he does know. When he discovers you are willing to let him sit until he comes up with a truthful answer, he will.

These are other unacceptable responses to questions you ask your kids:

- ✓ I'm not sure
- ✓ Possibly
- ✓ I think so
- ✓ Maybe
- ✓ Kind of
- ✓ Sort of
- ✓ Whatever

When kids give these types of responses, they are most likely lying, because they do know the truthful response and don't want to give it to you because they don't want to get into trouble. It is our opinion that before 7-8 years of age, while kids may not be willing to tell the truth, on the other hand, they don't always have the maturity to see these responses as lying either. At what age you take this on is up to you as you are the only one who truly knows what your child does or doesn't understand.

Kids with the Sanguine temperament are masters at giving these kinds of answers. Many of those we listed above we learned from our Sanguine daughter. Kids with the Choleric temperament will look you in the eye, tell you they don't know the answer to your question and dare you to disagree with them. Kids with the Phlegmatic temperament will just shrug their shoulder and not respond at all, and kids with the Melancholy temperament will burst into tears and blame it on somebody else. Again, understanding your child's **temperament** gives you valuable perspective which will assist you in training him.[1]

What Parents Can Do

What else can a parent do when working with their children to teach them to think for themselves?

1. **Be consistent**. Consistency is what it takes to effectively train your children's hearts to be teachable. With so much going on in everyone's lives, it is difficult to be consistently focused on training your children. Slow your life down.

   I (Carla) had gotten myself overbooked with things to do that were interfering with my relationship with my husband and kids. I was always getting ready for something I had to do or somewhere I had to go. Someone told me it helped them to write down all their commitments and projects and check the ones that someone else could do, then get them to do it! Pare down your commitments to the things you are truly gifted or talented in.

2. **Create an environment where your kids feel safe**. For the number one way to create an environment where you kids will feel safe, you have no further to look than at your marriage. If kids can tell their parents are happy with each other, if your marriage is relatively tension free (this doesn't mean you don't ever argue or fight), your kids will be too.

3. **Take on their bad attitude.** Parents tend to deal with the actions of their kids but let bad attitudes go. This is unfortunate because attitude comes from the heart. When kids are 8 years of age and older, they need to be corrected *more* for their attitude than for their action, for the attitude is what drives the action. This does not apply to younger children because they don't understand the motivation behind what they think, feel or do.

4. **Say what you mean and mean what you say.** If you are not going to deal with your children's sin issues, then don't say anything to them about them. If you say something about a sin issue, then you need to do something about it. Otherwise you are throwing words into the air and it doesn't matter where they land because your kids know you aren't going to do anything about them.

5. **Treat your children as individuals.** When parents talk to us, as soon as they compare the child they are concerned about with one of his siblings (friends or cousins), a red flag immediately goes up in our minds. Your children are individuals. Please treat them like they are. They do not each have the same talents or skill levels as their siblings or your best friend's kids do. They especially do not have the same temperament. The one who doesn't have much to say, yet didn't do his chores because he didn't want to or did the bare minimum just to get by is as rebellious as the one who tells you he is not going to do his chores and throws a fit.

6. **Understand your children's temperaments**. There are four basic temperaments:

   - The happy-go-lucky, easily distracted, exaggerating **Sanguine**
   - The born leader, needs to be in control, demanding **Choleric**
   - The perfectionistic, detail-oriented, moody **Melancholy**
   - The laid-back, stubborn and procrastinating **Phlegmatic**

A child's personality is the combination of his temperament blend plus his environment. The strengths and weaknesses of each temperament give valuable perspective to parents on the areas their children need specific training in.[2]

There's More!

We have covered a lot of information in this chapter on *why* and *how* asking questions of your kids' helps you get to the truth in a way lecturing never will. When you calmly ask questions of your child and listen to his responses instead of being defensive, your child will feel respected and valued because you are giving his opinion weight and are treating him like a person instead of someone you can boss around. Establishing respect with a child ups the chances of him or her wanting to continue to share with you their potential choices, plans, thoughts and dreams.

There's more on asking questions in the next chapter!

"When our son was seventeen years old, he was likeable, talented and respectful of us and others. People often told us he was a born leader and adults complemented his character. This all sounds great, however, at this time I (Beth) was becoming increasingly frustrated with him because at home, he was not completing responsibilities that required attention to detail on time. However, he had plenty of time for his Facebook friends, his Bible study group and his high school sports activities.

I got into the pattern of reminding him to complete his chores and I held him accountable for computer time. I was characterized by lectures which did not change his behavior. When I heard this teaching at a conference, I sensed asking questions that led to his taking ownership of his responsibilities would help us.

With the teaching in this book, I learned to ask questions that required our son to take responsibility rather than me telling or reminding him what to do. We removed freedoms he had until he re-established ownership of his responsibilities. In response, he acknowledged his priorities were out of whack and he started working on getting his things done. It is of interest that at the same time as things were improving at home, his high school sports skills, which had become sloppy on the field improved as well.

In a recent conversation with this now 22 year old son, I asked him about this time in his life. He said with my lecturing, he didn't think he had the freedom to fail and experience the consequences of the poor choices he made because I stayed on him until he finished whatever he was working on. He was gifted in many areas of his life and I wanted him to succeed in all of them. But, rather than allow natural and logical consequences to teach him a lesson, I tried to convince him with words.

He learned to expect a lecture but wasn't persuaded by them to change his behavior. I could see his weaknesses clearly, but I didn't see how I contributed to the problem. Thankfully, with the guidance and application of this teaching, we've both learned valuable lessons which have improved our relationship. We are grateful to the Links for their insights and practical guidance they have shared with us along our journey of parenting."

-Ed and Beth, Missouri

"So Jesus said,
'If you abide in my word, you are truly my disciples, and you will know the truth and the truth will set you free.'"
John 8:31-32

Chapter 9

Put Your Child's Thinking Cap On

*P*arker was excited to finally be in Middle School. He was feeling quite big for his britches, and it was showing at home. He was no longer consistent at getting things done let alone on time. He waited until he was reminded several times to start working on his chores or schoolwork.

He could no longer be counted on to get his bed made every day before he left for school, something he had been good at doing for years. His mom, looking for dirty clothes to do laundry one morning, found his on the floor of his room heaped in a pile under the bedding he tossed on the floor.

His parents thought he would settle back into their comfortable routine when he got adjusted to being at the middle school, but he didn't. The weeks went by and instead of getting better, Parker's lazy attitude and lack of follow-through with his responsibilities worsened. Realizing he was becoming characterized by this, his parents decided intervention on their part was necessary.

His parents waited for a time he was not in trouble and sat him down and asked him if he enjoyed being disrespectful and a slob. They wanted to know if it made him feel good when he put others down. (Again, when you are asking questions to get to the bottom of a situation, only ask one question at a time and wait for your child's answer.)

They asked him if he thought the family members treated him with respect, which he did. They asked him how he felt when his brother went into his room a few weeks prior to this conversation and was messing around on Parker's computer. Parker reminded them he didn't like that at all. They asked him why he was treating all of them with total disrespect, the same way his brother had treated him that day. They asked him to cite the verse that was their family motto, which he did.

"And as you wish that others would do to you, do so to them."
Luke 6:31

Parker hung his head with shame, and admitted he just wanted to be top dog. His parents opened their Bibles and read to Parker this passage in Matthew 28:20- 28 where the mother of the apostles James and John asked Jesus if they could sit on His right and His left sides for eternity. Jesus responded by saying,

"But whoever would be great among you must be your servant, and whoever would be first among you must be your slave, even as the Son of Man came not to be served but to serve."

Parker's parents asked him what he thought Jesus meant when He said, "He who is first must be a slave" to the people he is over. Parker told them that he thought it meant the person who was first needed to be kind to the ones under him and to help them in any way he could. His parents asked him if he had been doing that. He wasn't ready to answer, so he wouldn't look at them.

His parents quietly waited until he looked at them again, and they asked him the same question. They wanted to know if he was kind and helpful to others including his siblings when he didn't want to be. If he was only kind and helpful when he wanted to be, then it was no big deal to him. When you do what you don't want to do and do it with a good attitude, it builds up the character in your heart.

Parker's parents told him his siblings already looked up to him. They asked him if he was ready to show everyone in the family he was ready to be top dog by becoming their slaves. Admitting he would rather serve his family than be enslaved to them, Parker shared several things he needed to do to get his act together including apologizing to his family members. Over the next few days he proved to his parents and siblings he had gotten the message.

What can parents do? They can ask questions instead of lecturing. Do you see how much more productive this is?

Guide Their Thinking

When you are tempted to give one of your children a lecture, think of how to word what you want to say in questions that will guide him to where you want his thinking to go. Carla used to write down the points of her lecture, word them in questions, solidify them in her mind and then go talk to the child in trouble. After doing this for a few months, I remember her telling me she was finally starting to think in questions.

When it comes to asking questions, think of it this way. You want your questions to lead your child to the destination of honest admission. On the path along the way to the destination, you want

> *You want your questions to lead your child to the destination of honest admission.*

him to see what he has done wrong and why it is wrong. When he arrives at the destination, he should be willing to admit he was wrong, work through the repentance, forgiveness and restoration process and accept the consequence you have decided to give him.

Yes or No

If you are relaxed and non-confrontational as you ask your child questions, but he still won't give you straight answers, re-word them into questions that require a *"yes"* or *"no"* response.

If Parker had been giving his parents vague, evasive responses to their questions above, they would have re-worded them like this:

Instead of "How did it make you feel when your brother went into your room and played on the computer a few weeks ago?" it would be re-worded to "Did you like it when your brother went into your room and messed with your computer?"

Instead of "Why are you treating all the members of the family the same way your brother treated you?" it would be re-worded to "Do you want everyone in the family to be as angry with you as you were with your brother?"

Instead of "What do you think Jesus meant when He said to be first you get to be everyone's slave?" it would be re-worded to "To be top dog you get to show everyone you are ready to be their slave. Are you ready to be the slave to all of us?"

If your child refuses to answer these questions, tell him "That was a 'yes' or 'no' question and I want a 'yes' or 'no' response."

> *"But above all, my brothers, do not swear*
> *either by heaven or by earth or by any other oath,*
> *but let your 'yes' be yes and your 'no' be no,*
> *so that you may not fall under condemnation."*
> James 5:12

Expose the Sin

Jackson couldn't stay out of trouble. He was getting corrected for things he didn't do. He couldn't understand why his parents thought he had done them, and all of his pleas and explanations were not being listened to.

When 11-year-old Jackson and his 14-year-old brother, Aaron were arguing, his mom sent them to their rooms, and she would talk to them individually to find out what happened. Aaron was the oldest, so Mom went to him first.

One day Mom saw Aaron shake a fist at Jackson and tell him she wasn't going to believe it when Jackson tattled on him because he was her favorite and she always listened to him. She was curious how he came up with this notion, much less said it, so she sat Aaron down for a chat.

She asked him why he thought he was her favorite. At first, Aaron responded by telling her it was because he was the oldest. His mom could tell he was lying because he wouldn't look at her when he said it. She told him she knew he didn't believe that.

Next, he told her he was her favorite because his behavior was better than Jackson's. This was his second lie, and his mom knew it. She told him if she lined up all the times each of them got in trouble over the course of a week, it would come out to be pretty equal, so that wasn't true either, and she knew he was aware of this as well.

Aaron told his mom he was keeping track, and Jackson got in trouble twice as many times as he did every day. Mom counted this as his third lie.

Questions Expose Sin

Aaron's mom couldn't believe what she was hearing. She told Aaron he was making up nonsense, and needed to tell her why he thought he was her favorite. What had she done to give him this impression? Did she buy him more treats than she did Jackson? Did she take him fun places and leave Jackson at home? Did she give in to him more often when he wanted something? Aaron's response to all these questions was "no".

Aaron told her he didn't think she played favorites when it came to any of these things, because he knew she didn't. When his mom kept pressing him with questions, he finally admitted he said it to

Asking questions will expose the sin in your child's heart.

get Jackson's goat when he got mad at him. His mom had already figured this out, but she wanted to hear him say it and knew he needed to admit it to her.

She sent Aaron to sit on his bed and wait for her then went in to talk to Jackson. She asked him again what had happened in the last couple days when he got in trouble. Then she went in to Aaron and asked him to explain what had happened during this same period of time. Aaron got his facts mixed up because he didn't remember what he had told her before, so he told more lies, and she recognized them for what they were.

Mom went in to Jackson and apologized and asked his forgiveness for not listening to him, and asked him how she could make it right for giving him consequences he didn't deserve. Jackson said all he wanted was for her to listen to him, and she promised him she would.

After their mom shared with the boys' father what she had learned about Aaron, they both went in to talk with him and told him he had lost their trust since he lied so easily. They would never know when he was telling them the truth and he was going to have to figure out how to earn their trust back. After Aaron apologized to them and to Jackson, Dad gave him a consequence Aaron would not soon forget.

Asking questions will expose the sin in your child's heart. Aaron's parents had no idea lying was such a part of his character, and that he was willing for Jackson to take consequences that should have been his greatly troubled them.

What Are Your Kids Thinking?

Sadie's mom was disappointed when she found her bed unmade again. Mom was sure her 7-year-old daughter could remember to make her bed on her own, couldn't she? Mom called her sister, who had older kids, and she reassured her that yes, Sadie was old enough to remember to make her bed without constant reminders.

When Sadie got home from school, over snacks, her mom asked her what things she needed to do in the morning before she came down for breakfast. Sadie rattled them off without hesitation, and making her bed was on the list.

When her mom asked her why she kept forgetting to make her bed, Sadie, busy munching on her favorite cookie, told her mom she didn't forget, she just didn't like doing it. Sadie's mom explained to her that she was going to have to do things she didn't like to do her entire life, whether she wanted to or not, so she might as well start now.

Sadie looked at her mom and said it wasn't true. She didn't think her mom and dad did anything they didn't like to do. Sadie's mom couldn't believe what she just heard. She asked Sadie where this thought had come from.

Sadie just shrugged and said everyone she knew couldn't wait to be an adult so they could do what they wanted to do whenever they wanted to do it. If they didn't want to do something, they wouldn't have to do it.

"Everyone" turned out to be one of her friends who had shared this 7-year-old bit of wisdom with her. Her mom explained to Sadie what the real life truth in this matter was, sharing with her all the things she did every day that she didn't like to do, starting with making dinner.

This experience taught Sadie's mom she could never take anything for granted when she thought she knew what Sadie was thinking. She needed to be patient and ask questions to get the full story before she jumped to conclusions.

Mom asked Sadie if she would like to take over some of the things she didn't like to do so Mom would have more free time to do the things she did enjoy doing. Sadie decided making her bed was enough for her to do, and she would make it every day from now on.

Be Neutral

Once the sin is exposed, it usually reveals areas parents need to train their children in that are lacking. How on earth would Sadie's mom have ever guessed the reason Sadie wasn't making her bed if she had lectured her instead of asking direct questions? You might be surprised what you will learn when you start asking your children questions.

Please notice that Sadie's mom wasn't threatening her and she wasn't harsh with her. She had even made Sadie's favorite cookie in time for her snack. She stayed calm, and instead of lecturing her she asked the questions she had written down before Sadie got home from school. She also kept her response neutral when Sadie told her what her friend had said, which, we will admit is not always an easy thing to do.

Sometimes, if our kids looked anxious when Carla and/or I would sit one of them down to ask them questions to find out why they were or were not doing something, we would tell them they were **not** in trouble. We just needed to understand what their thinking was behind some of their actions.

Since we also sat them down and asked questions when their behavior was good, this statement usually relaxed them. You are not going to find anything out from tense, uptight kids.

Take Time to Listen

When one of us needed to go shopping or do errands, we often took one of our kids with us. We found our kids would bring things up they wanted to talk about or learn more about because being in the car was a neutral place to chat.

When the conversation in the car was headed in a direction which required our full attention, both Joey and I often put our to-do list aside for the moment and stopped somewhere to get a drink so we could just talk with our child. The things we found out in these conversations were often revealing and surprising in very good ways. We learned a lot about what was in our kids' hearts and minds, and we are glad we took the time to do so.

Finding the Truth

There are times you aren't sure if your kids are telling you the truth when you are asking them questions to get to the bottom of a situation. How can you know if they are? You need to become students of your kids. Study them and learn their tendencies. These are ways you can do this:

1. **Look in your child's eyes.** Do they look away from you or look down at the ground when you are talking to them? If they don't want to look you in the eye, you can be sure there is a reason they are trying to avoid eye contact with you.

"Your eye is the lamp of your body.
When your eye is healthy,
your whole body is full of light,
but when it is bad, your body is full of darkness.
Therefore be careful, lest the light in you

be darkness. If then your whole body
is full of light, having no part dark,
it will be wholly bright,
as when a lamp with its rays give you light. "
Luke 11: 34-36

2. **Look at their body language.** If they fidget, play with their hands, cross their arms over their chest, or put their hands on their hips for example, they are telling you they are hiding something or they are defiant and aren't going to listen to your instruction.

3. **Listen to their speech.** Are they talking fast, so you won't have time to think through their story, or are they talking so soft you can't hear them? I (Carla) was frustrated with our youngest daughter, Amy. I was constantly asking her to speak up or slow down when she talked. One day, fully exasperated with her for talking so softly I couldn't hear her; I told her if I had to ask her again to speak up she would get a consequence. She gave me a look of pure astonishment,

> *When kids apologize, they have humble and teachable hearts and they will accept their consequence without a fight.*

although she knew I would be true to my word. Once I decided something was going to be a certain way, I generally stuck to it and my kids were well aware of this.

The next time I started to ask her to speak up, I stopped myself and sent her to her room to sit on her bed until she was ready to apologize. She lost the privilege of speaking for a couple hours for her consequence as the freedom to talk was what she had misused. Do not give consequences until children apologize. When kids apologize, they have humble and teachable hearts and they will accept their consequence without a fight.

4. **Watch your child's attitude.** Is your child's attitude humble and teachable, or arrogant, accusing, and cocky? Aaron's attitude was what caught his mom's attention during that fateful talk she had with him. He was arrogant and superior in his tone and demeanor which caused her to listen more carefully to his stories about what had happened between him and Jackson. When she realized his facts were not the same as they had been the day before, she knew he was lying. If he had been telling the truth, the facts he shared the next day would have been the same.

When it comes to these four things, before you open your mouth to give your child an instruction, you already know what you are dealing with. If you see a hardness in your child's eyes and his hands are on his hip and he is standing with his legs apart, you might as well take him on right then for being disrespectful, for he isn't about to do anything you instruct him to do or honestly answer any of your questions.

If your child appears nervous and is looking at her shoes and won't look up at you, she is desperately trying to hide something and you might as well find out what she doesn't want you to know and deal with it. Taking your child on when you realize something is not right is more important than whatever instruction you were about to give him. You can get back to that when his heart is humble.

If you take it on when you see your child's body language is inappropriate, your child will understand his body language is what he is getting into trouble for, not a task he didn't complete. When issues pile up, it gets difficult to deal with them separately, which needs to be done for effective training of your child's heart. So take your child on at the first sign of disrespect and things will be easier to deal with.

How Issues Pile Up

Raelynn's mom had to call her name three times before she responded to her. Raelynn's arms were crossed over her chest when she came to stand before her mom. When she was told to take out the trash, 12 year-old Raelynn responded it was her brother's job and she wasn't going to do it.

Her brother was at ball practice, and because the trash was overflowing, her mom told Raelynn once again to take it out. Mom would deal with her son later for letting the trash get too full before he took it out, but Raelynn didn't need to know this.

Raelynn angrily took it out after her mom lectured her, telling her unless she obeyed she wasn't going to go with her friend's family to their lakeside cottage for the weekend. The trash spilled everywhere when Raelynn dumped it into the can in the garage.

Deciding her parents would think her brother was responsible when they saw this, she kicked the trash towards the wall of the garage, put the can in front of it and walked away. When she got back to the house, Raelynn angrily told her mom she wasn't doing her brother's chore again and went upstairs to change her shoes.

How many offenses did Raelynn need to apologize for? I counted eight, did you?

1. She had to be called three times before she responded – lack of respect for her mom
2. She stood with her arms crossed over her chest when her mom gave her the instruction to take out the trash – disrespectful towards her mom with inappropriate body language
3. In an angry tone, she refused to do what she was instructed to do – disobedience; challenge to her mom's authority
4. Her mom had to repeat the instruction – Raelynn should have obeyed the first time the instruction was given
5. She was angry and didn't take care to do the job right – disobedience for not doing the job completely
6. She kicked the trash out of the way instead of picking it up – Lazy
7. She put the can in front of the trash on the ground – deceitful
8. Raelynn told her mom she was not going to do her brother's chore again – disrespect, challenge to authority

Can you see by this example how taking Raelynn on when she didn't respond the first time she was called would have eliminated seven of these offenses??

A Better Way

Let's see how Raelynn's situation could have been handled differently. Mom calls Raelynn's name, knowing she could hear her but Raelynn didn't respond. Mom waits for a minute then goes to her daughter and tells her she needs to sit on her bed to get her heart right.

Raelynn knows she doesn't have the freedom to talk or get off the bed until she is willing to apologize for not going to her mom when she heard her name called.[1] Raelynn sat on her bed for forty minutes with her arms crossed over her chest. Her mom is frustrated, but knows she must give Raelynn the time it is going to take to get her attitude straightened out. Reminding herself it is Raelynn's **choice** how long she sits, not hers, Mom starts to fix dinner.

Raelynn finds her mom and tells her she is ready to apologize, but her tone is still harsh and disrespectful. Raelynn starts the apology by saying she didn't hear her mom call her name. She is sent back to her room to sit again for lying.

Raelynn sits for more than an hour and then went to her mom again to tell her she is ready to apologize. She said, "Sorry for not coming, I need you to forgive me. What did you want me to do so we can get this over with?" Sound humble?

Raelynn is told to go back to her room and not to come down until she is willing to apologize appropriately, which she knows how to do. She told her mom it was almost time for her friend's mom to pick her up for the weekend. Raelynn tells her mom she can get back to this when she gets home Sunday night.

Raelynn's mother asks her how long it has been since she first called her name. Raelynn tells her it has been a couple hours. Her mom asks her whose choice it is to take that long. Raelynn admits it was her choice. Asking Raelynn why her mood is so foul, she hedges, then tells her mom she found out at school the guy she has a crush on likes someone else. She wishes she was prettier so he liked her instead.

Parents Understand Too

When her mom asks her why she didn't tell her this when she got home from school, Raelynn tells her mom she didn't think she would understand. Raelynn's mom reminds her she was once a girl too, and had crushes before meeting Raelynn's dad. Mom went on to say she knows exactly how it feels to be rejected by a guy.

Raelynn's mom asked her what would have been easier–to trust her to understand how Raelynn felt or to pout for two hours. Raelynn said it would have been a lot easier if she told her mom when she got home from school what had happened and sought her mom's forgiveness. To make it right, Raelynn said she would do what her mom wanted her to do with a good attitude. Her mom asked her to take out the trash and come find her when she was done.

After Raelynn took out the trash, she found her mom and told her she was sorry again, and asked her how she could give her mom back the time she took from her while she pouted and refused to apologize respectfully. Her mom said Raelynn could give her two hours back with a willingness to do whatever she asked with a cheerful heart.

With a quiet voice, Raelynn told her mom she should lose the weekend with her friend as a consequence for her bad attitude and for challenging her mom's authority, especially since she said she expected to be able to go without making things right first.

The Joy of Restoration

Asking her what grace is, Raelyn responded by telling her mom it is a gift you don't deserve. Her mom agreed, and told her daughter the next time something upset her at school, she hoped Raelynn knew she could confide in her. Raelynn assured her mom she knew she could. Her mom went on to say she was giving her the gift of grace and was going to let her go for the weekend with her friend. Raelynn hugged her mom with a thankful heart and went on her way.

> *"For by grace you have been saved through faith.*
> *And this is not your own doing, it is the gift of God,*
> *not a result of works so that no one may boast."*
> Ephesians 2:8-9

We really hope you can see how wonderful it is to have resolution between you and your children, and how this restores peace to your home and more importantly, with God. Keeping the big picture in mind, you are training your children for their future marriages. Learning how to restore with family members now will give your kids the knowledge and skill to do it with their future spouses.

"We have two children, ages 17 ½ and 15 years. We thought things were going well. Our kids were getting good grades in school and our son did his homework without us having to check up on him. Two years ago things began to disintegrate when we noticed our son's grades started slipping.

In an effort to discover the root of these changes, we started conversations with our son by asking him questions. We were frustrated with his responses of "I don't know," "I'm not sure," "kind of," and so on. He was not outwardly disrespectful, but we definitely got the feeling he was thinking "Why are you questioning me? I've got this." His personality is the type that makes decisions on his own without consulting anyone.

My (Anne's) personality is such I will keep at it until I get the answers I am looking for. I did all the thinking and tried to get him to be responsible by constantly reminding him. His behavior didn't change but mine eventually did. I was tired of being the one doing all the thinking. I (Brian) was frustrated because I knew if we could talk things out with our son everything would work itself out, but the line of questioning Anne was perpetually throwing at our son was causing him to pull away from us.

We thank God for the mentoring relationship we have with Joey and Carla. After discussing things with them and hearing their observations, it became clear we were not requiring our son to search his heart and take a look at the way he was behaving. Our questioning was like an interrogation which put him in the position of defending himself. He knew he had made some poor choices and decisions but he didn't want to go back and deal with them so his heart was entrenched with sin. We provided a battleground that was convenient for him to fight. By doing this, he could focus on defending himself to us rather than face himself.

The Link's helped us to think in questions that would be effective in getting answers. Instead of accepting our son's answer of "I don't know," which we were doing, we learned to ask him when would he know, and waited for him to give us a time. He didn't have the freedom to do anything else until he "did know." Once he saw that we truly did want to understand what he was thinking and why he was making certain choices instead of passing judgement on him, he began to open up to us.

When we required him to search his heart by not letting him do anything before he appropriately answered our questions and we had better questions to deflect his flippant responses, we found he was motivated to do so and he was quite effective about it. As it turned out, he had made a huge decision without telling us about it. When he finally opened up to us about it, he realized he had been unfair to us to make such a decision without talking it through with us first. We shared our life experiences with him and through this and our questions, he discovered there were many flaws in his plan. Because of this breakthrough, now when situations come up he is willing to talk things out with us. Because he has embraced the Godly principles we have put into his heart, these life-changing discussions have created memories for a lifetime."

-Brian and Anne, North Carolina

114

"Do nothing from rivalry or conceit,
but in humility count others more significant
than yourselves.
Let each of you look not only to his own interests,
but also to the interests of others. "
Philippians 2:3-4

Chapter 10

The Why Questions

*T*ori was invited to spend the night with her best friend to celebrate her friend's birthday. Her mom had no problem letting 11 year-old Tori go. Tori was excited because boys had been invited to the party too. All the guests were going to meet at a pizza place then go play laser tag, after which the boys would go home. She wasn't sure her parents would let her go if they knew boys were invited, so she neglected to share this information with them.

When Tori's mom picked her up the next day, the mother of Tori's friend told her the party had gotten out of hand and they had to call the boys' parents to come get them and take them home.

On the drive home, Tori's mom asked her if she had a good time. Tori told her she had a great time but didn't get much sleep and needed a nap when she got home. Her mom asked her if she knew other girls were invited to spend the night. Tori said that she did, it was a birthday slumber party after all. Dreading the answer, her mom then asked her daughter if she knew boys were coming to the party. Tori told her she didn't know boys were going to be invited for pizza and games. If you were Tori's mom, would you believe her?

3 Types of Questions

One of the things we learned in the parenting class[1] we took and now lead is there are three types of questions your kids ask you.

The three type of 'Why' questions are:

1. **Curiosity** – "Why is the sky blue? Why is the grass green? Why, why, why?" These are simple, non-threatening questions. If you have a child with the Sanguine temperament, he can ask hundreds of these questions every day which will drive you crazy!

   I (Carla) used to tell our daughter Amy when we got in the car to go somewhere that she got three questions before we got to our destination. The first time I told her this she immediately said, "Only three?" My response to her was "That's one!" She clamped her hand over her mouth and didn't say a word until she had a question she could no longer hold in.

   I will readily admit doing this to save my sanity. What I didn't realize is she was learning to process her thoughts and to give priority to the questions she really wanted answers to. This was the beginning of teaching her discernment.

2. **Comprehension** – "Why does the sign say 45 MPH here and the sign by our house says 25 MPH?" "Why don't I have to go to school today?" A comprehension question seeks understanding. These questions are looking for the reason why. When kids ask comprehension questions, they usually have a teachable heart so parents should find time to answer them.

3. **Challenge**–"Why should I do what you tell me to do?" "Why should I do my homework when I already know this stuff?" When a child/teen asks a question in a challenging way, he is telling the person in authority he doesn't have

117

the right to tell him what to do and his heart is not teachable.

When you answer your child's question of challenge, you are opening the door to debate and nego-tiation. This often enflames parents and they cut the dia-logue off and begin to lecture in a harsh and angry tone which

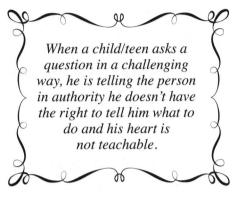

When a child/teen asks a question in a challenging way, he is telling the person in authority he doesn't have the right to tell him what to do and his heart is not teachable.

turns into a full-blown argument when their child responds to them. Never answer a challenge questions or you will be answering a "fool according to his folly" and become like him. You will be elevating him to a peer level with you.

"Answer not a fool according to his folly, lest you be like him yourself."
Proverbs 26:4

A lot of time, there was nothing wrong with the challenging question in and of itself, so let your child know when he comes to apologize if he asks it with a respectful tone, you will be glad to answer it.

The Stoplight

We want to give you a picture of what curiosity, comprehen-sion and challenging questions look like. You are driving to the store and stop at a red light. Your 4 year-old child is curious to know why the light is sometimes green and why it is some-times red. You tell her the different colors tell drivers what to do when they get to an intersection in the road. There is no harm in answering questions of curiosity.

At the next stoplight, your 6 year-old wants to know why you stop when the light is red and go when the light is green. Who told you to do this? You respond to this child by telling him you have to take a class and read a guidebook when you are learning how to drive and one thing you learn is what the colors tell all drivers to do. Parents should always answer comprehension questions, for when you do, you are teaching your child about something he is interested in.

Your 15 year-old says that he is not going to stop just because the light turns red if nobody is in the way. This wasn't a question, but rather a statement of challenge. You tell your teenager that he won't get his driver's permit until you and his dad can see his heart is teachable and he proves to you he can be counted on to be responsible.

What Parents Can Do When They are Challenged

So what else can you do when your child starts to challenge you? Walk away from the potential argument, telling your child you will talk about it with him when you both have had a chance to cool off. Cut the argument off before it gets started.

Our kids had to go to their room and sit on their bed with no freedom to do anything until their attitude changed, they were humble and teachable, and they were ready to answer the questions we asked honestly. When they came to us, they had to first apologize for challenging our authority.

If your kids won't stay on their bed or in a chair you tell them to sit in, then you need to work on obedience training with them. The first three chapters of our book, *"Why Can't I Get My Kids to Behave?"* tell how to do this.

Parents Take Control = Turn the Tables

When you are trying to get to the bottom of a situation with your kids, start the conversation with curiosity questions. Remember to stay calm! If you are angry, you are not starting a discussion, you are starting a war.

Tori's mom began a conversation with her when she picked her up from her friend's house. She asked her curiosity questions first, such as, did she have fun at the party, if she knew other girls were going to be there and if boys were going to be there.

Moving from curiosity to comprehension questions, Mom asked Tori why she didn't tell her other girls were being invited. Tori responded by saying she thought she had told her it was a slumber party. Her mom replied by saying a slumber party can be with just one friend or many. Tori said she didn't think when she was the only girl spending the night, it was considered a party.

Knowing anger would just start a power struggle with her child, Mom worked hard to stay calm as she asked comprehension questions. Mom asked Tori if she thought she would want to know all the other girls who were going to be at the party too.

Remember to stay calm! If you are angry, you are not starting a discussion, you are starting a war.

Tori told her she didn't think her mom needed to know who else would be there and asked why her mom didn't trust her, which told her mom what she wanted to know before she asked the rest of her questions.

"How were boys invited and you didn't know this? I am sure your friends talked about it for weeks before the party." This is the question that boxed Tori in. Her mom was right, she and her friends had been talking about it for weeks and were very excited boys had been invited to the party. She knew her mom would not believe any lie she told otherwise.

The difference between a parent asking a question for comprehension and one of challenge is in their **tone**. Because her mom's tone was calm, Tori admitted she knew boys were going to be there, but was afraid if her parents knew this they would forbid her to go.

Asking Questions is a Learned Skill

Learning to ask questions instead of lecturing your children is a skill. Here are some things to remember.

- Start your discussion when neither you or your child are angry — Don't ask questions when he has just been

caught and you are still fuming
- Use a calm voice
- Start with non-threatening (curiosity) questions to get him or her to open up
- Move into comprehension questions by asking him what he was thinking when he did whatever it was that got him into trouble
- Ask him what he could have done instead of what got him into trouble
- If any of the things he comes up with are acceptable, ask him if you can trust him to do it the next time he is faced with the same temptation
- If he says you can, have him write it down in his prayer journal so he can look at it every day and ask God to help him be strong enough to use the way out he came up with

We have tried to encourage you to see that asking questions of your kids to get to the root of the issue will eliminate any need to lecture them.

Jesus Asked Questions Too

Did you know in the four Gospels in the New Testament, Jesus asked over 150 questions? As you read through the stories in the New Testament, you see Jesus asked questions to get people to **think**. What a great example this is to us!

*Jesus asked questions to get people to **think**.*

The most important question you will ever ask your child when you know he is mature enough to understand what Jesus did when He died on the cross for us is, "Who is Jesus?" This will open a discussion to talk about Jesus to see if your child is ready to accept Christ as his/her personal Lord and Savior if he hasn't already done so.

Please don't assume asking this question is the responsibility of your child's Sunday School teacher, mid-week children's activity leaders or youth leaders. Don't you want to be the one to pray with your child or teen when he/she gives his life to Christ?

"Monica and I have been married for 25 years and we have 8 children ages 21 to 2. We have been using these principles for over 18 years.

The 3 types of questions a child can ask as outlined in this book have been of great value to us in our parenting. When we realize what type of questions our children are asking, it allows us the understanding of how to respond. They have allowed us to respond without anger in many cases and saved us hours of time in not getting into lecture talks. The personalities of each child are different and asking the three "Why" questions works for each of them.

We have also learned to ask questions of our children in order to get to the truth and discern the truth as they go through the various phases of growing up. Keeping our tone appropriate makes a world of difference!"

-Jim and Monica, Texas

"For God so loved the world that He gave His only Son, that whoever believes in Him should not perish but have eternal life."
John 3:16

Chapter 11

Children Can Escape Temptation

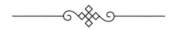

$\mathcal{W}$e were scheduled to speak at a parenting conference seven hours away from home. Our son, then 15 years-old wanted to stay home alone as he needed to participate in the high school marching band at the Friday night football game while we were gone.

I (Joey) could only think of all the bad things that could happen while we were gone. What if the house caught on fire or the warning siren went off signaling a potential tornado in the area? What would he do when his band friends, knowing we were gone, came over after the game ready to party, even though they knew Michael didn't drink? Would he drink, thinking he wouldn't get caught?

Before I could open my mouth, Michael went on to say that when he thought of the worst case scenarios that could happen, he knew the one we would be most concerned about would be his friends in the marching band coming over after the football game and bringing alcoholic drinks with them. We often had the band kids over for pizza and to watch the video I taped of the half-time show they performed in. This was an outreach project of ours (the kids wouldn't think of bringing alcohol when we were there however), so it would not be unusual for them to think it was okay to come whether we were home or not.

We had been working with Michael for some time on planning ways of escape for things that came up, and this was a time he showed us he knew how to prepare for one very well. He had thought through what could go wrong regarding the worst case scenarios he had come up with and had made wise decisions regarding a potentially compromising situation.

He had already made arrangements with a police officer friend of ours who lived close by. If his friends came to the house, without letting them inside, he would tell them this officer was expecting him to come over for the evening, and he would get on his bike and go. If this happened, our friend did expect him to come, so this was not a lie. Given all this, how could we not let him stay home?

Proactive planning for acceptable "ways of escape" gives both parents and kids peace of mind. By the way – this officer decided to stop by and pick Michael up and take him to a movie. When he got there, a car full of rowdy guys had just pulled into our driveway. Perfect timing!

> *"No temptation has overtaken you that is not common to man.*
> *God is faithful, and he will not let you be tempted*
> *beyond your ability, but with the temptation,*
> *he will also provide the way of escape,*
> *that you may be able to endure."*
> I Corinthians 10:13

The Way of Escape

What is a "way of escape"? It is a means of escaping a situation where you are being tempted to do something wrong.

When kids know in advance what an appropriate way of escape is, they are much more likely not to give in to temptation.

The time to think of a way of escape is not when you are being tempted. We worked with our kids from the time they were around eight years old to think of ways of escape in advance. Because Michael had a good way of escape planned in the scenario above, when the kids got there he had a plan of action ready even if our friend had not stopped by to pick him up for a movie.

What would Michael have done if a car-load of kids armed with cases of beer pulled into the driveway and pushed their way into the house? Chances are they would have ignored any plea he made not to drink. If the party had gotten out of control and the neighbors had called the police, Michael knew we would be in trouble. How much better it is to teach your kids what a way of escape is and work with them on planning them so they know how to come up with them on their own.

According to I Corinthians 10:13, we will not be tempted in a way we cannot avoid. This means there is *always* a way of escape available to us and our children at any given moment in time.

Part of giving ownership of behaviors and responsibilities to children of any age is to teach them to proactively find ways of escape. When kids know in advance what an appropriate way of escape is, they are much more likely *not* to give in to temptation. When your kids learn how to resist temptation by taking a way of escape, they will stay out of trouble.

Little Ones are Tempted Too

When our daughter Amy was 2 years-old, she loved to pull the photo albums off the shelves, take the pictures out and "love" Mommy and Daddy as she squeezed the life out of the pictures she was holding to her cheeks. The temptation to "love" the pictures was stronger for this little girl than my warning not to touch the albums.

I was horrified, but knew I could not yell at her. I needed to yell at myself for leaving the albums where she could get to them. She was too young to resist this powerful of a temptation. So what did my warning of "Don't touch" and the lecture she got when I caught her mean? It meant absolutely nothing. Don't allow young children to be tempted when they don't have the maturity to resist.

> *Don't allow young children to be tempted when they don't have the maturity to resist.*

Parents are the "Way of Escape" for Their Little Ones

Parents need to provide a way of escape for their young children. I could have given Amy a way of escape by keeping the photo albums in a cupboard where she could not reach them, and I should have done this.

Your 3 year-old is out of control. He is hitting his younger brother whenever he gets mad at him, which is most of the time. He throws a fit during naptime and won't stay in bed. He asked for a peanut butter and jelly sandwich for lunch, and then throws it on the floor when you give it to him. Where is the way of escape in all of this?

Look at your family's schedule. In the past week, how many times has your son gotten to bed at his regular time? Has he had a nap in his bed every day or in the car seat while you are doing errands? Has he been in too many situations where he is over-stimulated (non-structured play times with other kids, a few afternoons with his over-indulgent grandma, attended too many events)? If this sounds familiar, you have an over-tired child on your hands.

What is this 3 year-old's way of escape? You are. Over-tired toddlers and preschoolers are not going to behave. He can't control his behavior and he shouldn't be expected to.

Parents, it is your job to stand in front of your young children and pave the way for them, eliminating temptations in their path. It is your responsibility to protect them by keeping them out of situations where they are not able to keep themselves under control. They will have plenty of opportunities every day to exercise self-control when it is possible for them to do so.

> *"And He said to His disciples, 'Temptations to sin are sure to come, but woe to the one through whom they come! It would be better for him (or her) if a millstone were hung around his neck and he were cast into the sea than he should cause one of these little ones to sin. Pay attention to yourselves!"*
> Luke 17:1-2

Kids (6-10 Years) and the "Way of Escape"

Parents of a 3rd grader recently told us he was frequently getting into trouble at school. Another boy was teasing him all the time and doing things to provoke him and trouble ensued. The other boy was sneaky and he didn't get caught. These parents told us their son's outbursts of frustrated anger did not go unnoticed by the school staff, however.

Mom and Dad worked with their son to find a way of escape. They believed their son came up with a sound plan, so all three of them went to see his teacher. Their son asked his teacher if he could stay inside during recess when things got bad and help the teacher or read. The teacher agreed to this and the boy stayed out of trouble for a week.

When his teacher realized this, she sent him back to recess and she watched where she could not be seen by the kids at play. She saw the bully teasing and provoking this child once again, and stepped in to deal with him.

What can you learn from these parents?

- ➤ They asked their son to come up with a way of escape, knowing he would take ownership of it if it was his idea.

- ➤ If he couldn't come up with one, his parents had one ready.

- ➤ Their son did come up with a plan. Even though it was not the way of escape his parents had thought of, they still supported their son's plan to show him they believed he could initiate ways of escape himself.

- ➤ They showed their son their emotional and physical support by going with him to talk to the teacher.

- ➤ Every day they asked him how he was handling the time he spent inside during recess. They encouraged him for sticking to the way of escape.

> ➢ Their son's way of escape also showed the teacher he was not the trouble-maker.

Best and Worst-Case Scenarios

Avoiding temptation when it presents itself in a package that a teenager cannot resist opening is almost impossible, or so it seems. Teens are more susceptible to temptation when they don't have a good relationship with their parents and they don't feel like they fit in at home, school, or church.

When we worked with our kids when they were teens to pro-actively find a way of escape, we would have them write down three best-case scenarios and three worst-case scenarios. We would have them write a way of escape for each of the worst-case scenarios. This is how Michael had a way of escape ready when he talked to his dad about staying home alone.

"But each one is tempted when, by his own evil desire,
he is dragged away and enticed.
Then, after desire has conceived, it gives birth to sin;
and sin, when it is full-grown, gives birth to death."
James 1:14-15

Eve Isn't the Only One Who Ate the Apple

Who tempts us? Satan does. He makes sure what he is tempting us with looks really, really good. He uses our friends and other resources to do so. He does his best to get us to give in. When we do, he gets to look triumphantly at God and say, "I told you so!"

"Put on the whole armor of God, that you might be able to
stand against the schemes of the devil."
Ephesians 6:11

It's Not Avoidable

God says you will be tempted. So will your children. This is an unavoidable fact of life. He also says He understands the power of temptation and where it can lead to, and He is with you every step of the way. Think about it! God is with you **every** single time you or your child is tempted and He will help you find and utilize a way of escape. What a relief! There is never a time when we or our children are tempted that there is **_not_** a way of escape. Never!

*God is with you **every** single time you or your child is tempted and He will help you find and utilize a way of escape.*

Have you ever told your kids this? What a life-long gift you give your children when you train them to find a way to escape instead of giving in to temptation.

"The principles that Joey and Carla have explained so practically in this chapter are "spot on". When our four children were young, we intentionally started teaching them right from wrong. As they have grown and matured over the years we have had more and more discussions about facing temptations. We have found that talking through possible ways to escape temptation is most valuable when done during times of non-conflict.

When our children were younger and were first being asked to stay overnight at a friend's house, we were hit with the reality that our kids would most likely face temptations without us. Would they make wise choices and be strong enough to stand up on their own? Well, as you might guess, we certainly saw some successes and some failures over the years. The successes enabled us to encourage them while the failures gave us great opportunities for more training so that they could make better decisions the next time.

Joey and Carla taught us to ask probing questions when our teens make foolish choices rather than lecture them. It is critical for us to have them search their own hearts and then take full responsibility for the resulting outcome. They take part in the process of choosing an appropriate consequence for their actions, and they are encouraged to explain how they will handle things differently in the future. This provides them with a way out the next time temptations comes.

Teaching our children to find a way of escape when tempted and helping them to understand the power of the full armor of God (Ephesians 6:10-17) are key elements to their growth in making wise choices in life. We are so grateful that we have been able to successfully apply these principles with our children."

-Kurt and Jill, Ohio

"Do not be conformed to this world,
but be transformed by the renewal of your mind,
that by testing you may discern what is the will of God,
what is good and acceptable and perfect. "
Romans 12: 2

Chapter 12

Getting Your Child to Own His Behavior

I (Carla) was starting the coffee while Joey sat up some portable chairs. I could see cars turning into our driveway through the kitchen window. People came into the house, laughing and talking. It was a normal Tuesday night in our home. Joey and I were leading a parenting class. After the opening group discussion, we settled into chairs in the hallway to listen to the video presentation. Even though we had led this class many times, we still heard things in a new way as our kids were older and at different levels of maturity than the last time we had taught the class.

Tucked into some great teaching was the phrase,

"With responsibility comes freedom."

I am not sure I had ever heard this phrase before! I even asked Joey if the videos had been revised. We looked at each other and said, "If Michael is so irresponsible, why does he have so many freedoms?!"

We made a list of his responsibilities and gave him a grade on how well he consistently did each one without reminders from us. Then we listed his freedoms. Not only did he fail his responsibility report card, the total number of freedoms versus the responsibilities he had was about three to one. No wonder he didn't get his stuff done! He didn't have to because he was having a great time with all the freedoms and privileges he had.

Play Ball, Yes or No?

It wasn't long after this revelation that Michael got a call from a friend to play basketball one Saturday. Joey was out of town, so Michael asked me if he could go. Usually I would have gone through the list of all the things I knew he had been told to do, asking if he had completed each of them. I have no idea how this statement came out of my mouth, so it must have been a "God-thing".

I said, *"Do you have the freedom to go?"*

He looked at me for a minute and then started listing the extra chores his dad had given him to complete plus his normal chores, none of which had been started, and finished by saying he had a paper due in school on Monday he hadn't started to work on either.

I thought to myself, "He knows exactly what he is supposed to do, so why do we keep reminding him?!"

Then he said, "So, can I go?"

I am sure I gave him a stupefied look as I thought to myself, "He has to be kidding me! Why would he ask me such a ridiculous question?"

After a minute I said, "You just told me all the things you have to do this weekend. Why on earth would you ask me if you could go?"

Michael shrugged and said, "If you say 'no', then I will argue with you until you give in, and if you say 'yes', when Dad gets on me for not getting the chores done, I will tell him you said I could go, and he will be mad at you instead."

He was right. This was exactly what had happened countless times in our home and would again unless something changed.

Please don't ever second guess yourself where your kids are concerned. They know *exactly* what they are doing and why! Instead of yelling at him (which I certainly wanted to do), instead of giving him a scathing lecture (which I had already composed in my head), I said, "I am going to let you decide if you have the freedom to go."

Who Decides?

"I am going to let you decide if you have the freedom to go."

I have no idea where this came from either. After I made this statement, all I could think about was how much trouble I would be in with my husband if Michael made the wrong decision. I could tell I was onto something however, when I looked at Michael and saw the puzzled expression on his face.

Michael told me it was my decision to make, not his. The more he demanded I make the decision, the more I knew I needed to wait for him to make it. Too many times when kids press their parents for a decision that requires a "yes" or "no" answer, we give them one without thinking things through. Let your kids think it through and see if they come up with a wise and mature response.

This started a revolution in our home. After this fateful day, our response to our kids when they asked us to do something was, "Do you have the freedom to?"

I did not give in, and Michael finally called his friend and told him he had too much stuff to do and he didn't have the *freedom* to play ball.

This started a revolution in our home. After this fateful day, our response to our kids when they asked us to do something was, "Do you have the freedom to?"

No matter which child was standing before us, he/she would list all he had yet to do and respond by saying, "No, I will go get my stuff done now."

By asking them this question, we no longer needed to lecture or remind them. The tables had finally been turned. We were no longer frustrated, but our kids certainly were!

No Magic Bullet

Now, before you put this book away thinking we have given you a magic bullet to use with your kids, first of all, asking your kids if they have the freedom to do something is age-appropriate. Children under 6-7 years of age will most likely not understand what you are saying if you ask them if they have the freedom to do something.

It's all in how you word your question. 4 year-old Mia's mom told her to put her dolls away. Mia starts playing with something else and didn't get this task done. Later on, she asks her mom if she could go outside and play.

Instead of saying, "Did you get your dolls picked up?" her mom asked her, "What did I ask you to do earlier?"

If Mia responded by saying, "I don't know," her mom would have had her sit for a few minutes without the freedom to speak until she did know. When Mia told her mom she was told to put her dolls away, her mom asked her if she had completed this task. When Mia admitted she had not, her mom told her she could not give her permission to go outside until her dolls were put on the shelf where they belonged.

Obedience Summary

Asking your children if they have the freedom to do something is not going to work on a consistent basis unless you have trained your kids to obey you.

As a reminder of what obedience training looks like:

Kids need to be taught to obey -

- When you call them (immediately)
- How they are instructed to do a task (completely)
- Without arguing with you (challenging your authority)
- Without complaining (complete the task with a good attitude)

Once your kids are trained to obey when you give them an instruction, how you have told them to complete the task, without arguing with you and without whining or complaining while they are doing what you told them to do, they will give you an honest answer when you ask them if they have the freedom to do something.

For little ones, another way of saying this is they need to do what you have told them to do, "Right away, all the way, with a happy heart." They don't have the maturity to understand the reason their heart is not happy. Once they are in elementary school, 'happy heart' looks different because they know if they are challenging your authority (arguing with you) or if they just don't want to do it (whining and complaining).

Review–It's About Ownership

When you lecture your kids, you are taking ownership of what is on their "to-do list". You are telling them what to do so it is up to you to see that they do it. When you ask your child a question such as, "Do you have the freedom to...?" you are giving him ownership of getting his stuff done.

Look again at the question 4-year-old Mia was asked in the scenario above. If her mom has asked her if she had put her dolls away yet, Mom would be taking ownership of the dolls getting put away because even though she worded it in a question, she was reminding Mia what she was told to do.

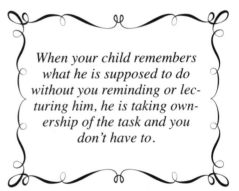

When your child remembers what he is supposed to do without you reminding or lecturing him, he is taking ownership of the task and you don't have to.

Mia's mom worded her question, "Mia, what did I ask you to do?"

This change in the way the same question was worded gave ownership of putting the dolls away to Mia, where it belonged. When Mia responded by telling her mom she was told to put her dolls away, Mia was "remembering" what she needed to do instead of her mom remembering for her.

When your child remembers what he is supposed to do without you reminding or lecturing him, he is taking ownership of the task and you don't have to. When a parent is doing all the remembering, ownership of the task is squarely in that parent's lap.

When parents remind their older children to do something, they are keeping ownership of the task as well. When 9-year-old Evan's dad asked him what homework he has to get done, Dad took ownership from Evan of getting his homework done because Dad will take it upon himself to remind Evan to do it and Evan knows it.

The next morning before he leaves for work Dad goes through Evan's homework assignments and didn't see any math papers. When Evan tells his dad he didn't get it done, Dad launches into yet another lecture which started with, "How many times have I told you to get all your schoolwork done before you go to bed?"

"How many times have I told you...?"

Who has the ownership of getting the schoolwork done? Ultimately it is still your child's responsibility, but he doesn't have to plan when he is going to do it as long as you are willing to assume that responsibility for him by repeatedly reminding him to get it done.

Your child will mess around doing what he wants to do until your tone of voice reaches a certain decimal level, at which time he will buckle down and get the bare minimum amount of homework competed. Rarely will he have any intention of doing all his homework and doing it well until he can tell by your tone of voice and body language he has pushed you over the edge. Substitute chores for homework in a similar scenario, and we trust you are getting the picture here.

Owning It

How do you know when it is appropriate to transfer ownership of a particular behavior to one of your children?

This child needs to:

> ➤ Be obeying you a good percentage of the time
> ➤ Be handling the behaviors you have already given him

➢ Have his schedule under control–giving it to him should not overwhelm him. He should not have a lot of activities or upcoming events on his plate like a baseball tournament his team is in or a paper due at school.

When parents verbally transfer ownership of a behavior to one of their children, they need to ask this child:

- What behaviors is he now responsible for
- How he is going to manage this behavior on his own
- What he needs to do if he needs help
- What will happen if he fails to manage it properly

Asking these types of questions gets both you and your child on the same page, and makes it easier to know what to hold him accountable for if he doesn't follow through at some point.

No More Reminding

Reminding your kids to get their stuff done is the flip side of lecturing. You are taking ownership of their responsibilities on both ends. You are either reminding them of the task before they have attempted to do it, or you are lecturing them about it after you find out they haven't done it.

Reminding your kids to get their stuff done is the flip side of lecturing.

Once again, it is all about you, the parent doing all the remembering, so your child knows he doesn't have to.

Reminding + Lecturing = Parental Ownership

Painful Motivation

The most effective way to give ownership of their responsibilities to your children is to give them consequences when they give it back to you. We think the number one reason parents lecture is because they don't know what else to do. Another word for "what else to do" is ***consequences***.

137

When your kids keep proving to you they have no intention of completing tasks and chores they don't want to do until they are forced to, you are going to have to give them a consequence to motivate them to stay on task. Kids need pain to get them to do what they don't want to do.

Again, no lecture delivers pain. While we are blowing off steam, our kids tune us out, thinking of what is going to happen the second Tuesday of next month. Meanwhile, we think we are getting our point across in no uncertain terms, and things will change.

When things don't change, it is time for consequences. Parents often have difficulty thinking of an appropriate consequence to give. The ones you think of when you are angry are often not appropriate for the situation, and when your spouse finds out what you dished out, he/she will let you know how unreasonable you were in front of the children and that makes you angry all over again.

For consequences to be effective:

- They must be painful
- They must be given consistently
- They must be given at the first sign your kids show they have no intention of doing what they have been told to do

Consequences Need to Hurt

If you are unwilling to give your child consequences that will cause him enough pain to motivate him to follow through with his responsibilities, how will he learn to do so, and what is the point of giving them in the first place?

The amount of pain your child needs is, of course age-appropriate. If your 3 year-old will not pick up his toys, he loses the freedom of playing with them for his consequence. Fifteen minutes of sitting in a chair with nothing to do is going to seem like an eternity to a 3 year-old child.

When an 8 year-old child won't pick up his toys, fifteen toy-less minutes is not going to cause him any pain. Having no toys to play with the rest of the afternoon, however, will seem endless.

When your teenager won't pick her stuff off the floor of her room, put it in an empty laundry basket and put it in the closet of your room for three days. No matter how much she needs the stuff in the basket, she goes without it. Are you getting the picture of what pain looks like?

Parents really are softies at heart, and don't want to see their children suffer. Think of it this way – did you give your child the opportunity to get the task done? Of course you did. Who chose not to do it? Your child did. You certainly didn't force him not to follow through with your instructions. If you don't give painful consequences, how else are you going to teach your kids to do what they are told or know they are supposed to do when they are told to do it?

They Lose What They Misused

The most effective consequence to use when your kids don't get a responsibility done on time or are not using the moral character values you are teaching them is the loss of a freedom or privilege. In other words, they lose the privilege of whatever they were **misusing**. While lectures don't change inappropriate behaviors, the loss of a privilege certainly does.

Connor was watching television and didn't get the trash taken out. He loses the freedom of watching television because he was misusing the privilege of watching it.

The first thing all kids want to know is *"For how long?"*

If they are over 6 years of age, ask your kids what they have to do to get/earn it back. Connor said he has to do his chores before he watches television. His parents told their 9 year-old son they needed to see him take the trash out (with no reminders and with a good attitude) on a regular basis before he would get the freedom of watching television back.

When one of your children loses the freedom of a privilege, don't give him a time-frame for when he will get it back. You should have one in mind, like a couple weeks for Connor's situation, but don't tell your child this. Connor's parents watched him to see if he took the chore of getting the trash out seriously.

It you give them their freedoms back too soon, they will do what they have to do just to get it back, but no longer. So give them time to get into the habit of taking the trash out for example. If Conner whined and complained during this time, his parents would let him know he extended it a day every time he whined. This effectively takes care of the complaining problem.

Keep the Ball in Their Court

The "loss of a freedom" or privilege replaces grounding your kids. When you ground your child from watching television for example, you give him a time limit. When you do this, he just serves the time. It is easier for your child to serve the time given when grounded than it is for him to take on the responsibility of *earning* that privilege back.

By not giving your child a time limit when you take the privilege of a freedom away, you are putting the burden of his lack of responsibility back on him. By giving him ownership of his responsibilities by having him earn back the freedom he lost, you are throwing the ball back in your child's court.

Your children want to keep the ball in your court. Believe it or not, they would rather play defense than offense. When the ball is in your court, all they have to do is decide if they are going to obey or not. Don't let your children make their rebellion about you. Your children know why they lost the freedom of something important to them.

It's Your Child's Problem

When you have decided to take away the privilege of what your child is misusing, ask yourself, "What *is* this child misusing?"

Go beyond the surface and look for the root issue. We know of a family who has four boys. They were homeschooling, and Mom was frustrated with all the pushing, shoving and hitting that occurred each day, every day. They thought they had taken away everything important to their boys.

During a chat this mom and I (Carla) were having about this, I asked her what the boys were misusing. She decided they were misusing their hands. She took away the freedom of using their hands, and told them to keep them in the pockets of their jeans, yet they still had to get their schoolwork and chores done. When they asked her how they were supposed to do this, she shrugged and told them she had no idea, but it wasn't her problem.

She asked them how many times she had told them to quit shoving each other. They admitted she had been telling them for years. She let them know she thought she had given them plenty of time to show her they would use their hands appropriately, and asked them if they agreed.

They couldn't disagree, so she told them they had left her no choice but to take their hands away since they would not use them wisely. They were the ones who used their hands in inappropriate ways, and they were the ones who had to figure out how to get their stuff done without them. Needless to say, one "handless" day was long enough for these boys to figure out another way to tease each other.

Stop Lecturing! Stop Reminding!

When your kids are not responsible, give them ownership of their responsibilities by holding them accountable when they don't get their stuff done. No more lectures and no more reminders. If you need to get a higher percentage of obedience from them, then get to work on that first. Remember, kids need to be responsible before they can enjoy freedoms.

In Summary

So, in summary, the key to stop reminding and lecturing your children is:

1. Train them to obey you and all authority figures in their lives
2. Teach them to think for themselves by asking questions
3. Give them ownership of their responsibilities

    4.   Teach them how to pro-actively plan for a way of escape when faced with temptation

What Parents Can't Do

Parents can't get into the heart of their child. You can put information, instruction and knowledge into your child's heart. You can spend time with your child showing him how to put what he has learned into practice. You can provide external consequences that will motivate your child to choose behaviors that are moral and right. But, you cannot make the choice within the heart of your child to do right over wrong. Only your child can do this.

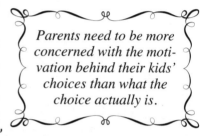

Parents need to be more concerned with the motivation behind their kids' choices than what the choice actually is. While the choice is important, it's not nearly as important as the **"why"** they made the choice. Yes, we are back to the *what* and the *why*. We encourage you to look at why your child is making wrong choices instead of lecturing him for what the choice was.

Parents need to be more concerned with the motivation behind their kids' choices than what the choice actually is.

All too often parents give consequences for the **"what"** when they should be teaching into the **"why".** If the "why" is not Godly (moral), then it is wrong, and it would be dangerous to allow your child or teen to work off it.

Parenting to the Future

Parenting with the goal of training our children to be responsible is parenting with an eye to the future. We are raising our children to be responsible adults. Parenting our children with an eye to the future allows us to rise above what can seem like the daily grind of training, instructing and disciplining them. Parenting our children with an eye to the future requires forward thinking on our part, which includes planning and evaluating.

Parenting with an eye to the future means we have a clear picture of the character we are trying to build into our children. Parenting with an eye to the future means parents understand they have a job to do which their children will likely resist, but the parent who perseveres, keeping the long-term goal in mind will see their children shine representing God to the world in a big way.

"We learned the principles and truths in this chapter early on in our parenting. We have four sons who are now all young adults who love the Lord with all their hearts and who do not hesitate to stand firm on the truths of God's Word.

With four active boys in our home while they were growing up, we were driving each other nuts trying to remember if each boy was caught up with all his schoolwork and chores. We will never forget the conversation we had with Joey and Carla when they revealed to us our need to transfer ownership of our boys' actions and behaviors to them.

"Why are you reminding them?" Joey asked us. Beth Ann carefully explained they weren't following through on their responsibilities. "Why aren't they following through with their responsibilities?" was Joey's next question. We responded by saying they didn't follow through because they didn't want to do them. Joey's final question was "What are you doing to make them want to complete their responsibilities?" Beth Ann and I looked at each other and could not come up with an answer for this question. Joey and Carla started talking and we did some serious listening.

By transferring ownership of their behaviors and actions to our children, we taught them how to think for themselves and required them to act on the values we were instilling in their hearts. When we would throw the ball back into their court, they would pick it up, decide what to do with it and more often than not come up with an appropriate response. If we had chosen to keep the ball in our court; reminding, nagging, lecturing and so on would become the order of the day. What a burden that is for us as parents. Using questions like the ones Joey asked us before we got frustrated with our sons, we kept throwing the ball back at them until they picked it up and did something with it!

Throwing the ball back in their court gives you the freedom to hold them accountable for their actions by coming up with appropriate consequences or by asking them if they need and want your assistance in discussion or action. Holding our kids accountable for what they have been taught challenged their mind, will and emotions to do the right thing. Helping our boys do the right thing for the right reason opened the door for future conversations where they learned to embrace the foundations of our faith in their heart, soul, mind and action.

We worked hard to instill biblical values in their hearts. To leave it there instead of them thinking through how to apply those values would be like teaching them to drive without ever letting them take the wheel. How would they ever understand how the world works and become responsible citizens without this kind of training? How would they ever learn to live by God's principles in any given situation?

Next to obedience training, learning how to transfer ownership to our children in this way was the most helpful and most used tool in our parenting toolbox. We are forever grateful to Joey and Carla for teaching this to us."

-Chuck and Beth Ann, Pennsylvania

"Be very careful, then, how you live –
not as unwise, but as wise; making the most
out of every opportunity."
Ephesians 5:15-16

Appendix A

Unlocking Your Child's Heart

The Repentance, Forgiveness and Restoration Process

"I'm Sorry" isn't Enough

Kids need to learn what repenting looks like, for this is the key to unlocking your child's heart. When I (Carla) was growing up, my mom used our home to host Child Evangelism Fellowship Backyard Bible Clubs. I can still remember the words to the song about "repentance" saying you turn around in a U-turn and go the other direction. To "***repent***" means confessing your sin with the intent of not repeating it.

> *"For godly grief produces a repentance that leads to salvation without regret, whereas worldly grief produces death."*
> *2 Corinthians 7:10*

'Godly grief' leads a person to ask the one they have offended for ***forgiveness***. Asking for forgiveness ***restores*** the relationship, just as Jesus restored our relationship with Him when we ask Him for forgiveness of our sins.

'Worldly grief' apologizes by saying "I'm sorry." The only thing kids are sorry for is they got caught, and they will do it again as soon as you turn your attention to something else. Young children are not able to know what worldly grief is and "I'm sorry" works for them until they understand the power of repentance Jesus gave us by dying on the cross, usually around the age of 7-9 years.

After that, they need to repent, seek forgiveness and do what it takes to restore the relationship. Repentance and worldly grief are not compatible.

"For by grace you have been saved through faith.
And this is not your own doing. It is a gift from God,
not of works so that no one may boast."
Ephesians 2:8-9

The third part of the repentance process is **restoration**. The one asking for forgiveness shares how he will ***give back*** what he took away. We taught our kids to ask the person how they could make it right when they were first learning this process. Once they understood what "making it right" looked like to others, instead of asking how they could make it right, they had to come up with a way to do it and say, "This is how I am going to make it right."

When 7 year-old Austin apologized to his 3 year-old sister for grabbing her toy, he told her he was going to make it right by letting her play with her favorite toy of his. When 11 year-old Sallie apologized to her 9 year-old sister for saying something untrue about her to friends, she told her to make it right she was going to go to her friends and tell them she had made it up.

Paul is speaking to Christians —

"Finally brothers, rejoice. Aim for restoration,
comfort one another, agree with one another,
live in peace; and the God of love
and peace will be with you."
1 Corinthians 13:11

When we first worked with our kids on teaching them the repentance process, we were dismayed that they were not putting it into practice at home unless we forced them to. Carla came up with this neat idea to teach them the process during one of our family nights, and it worked. Our children began taking ownership of asking for forgiveness after that.

The Repentance, Forgiveness & Restoration Process

Things you need:

1. Red poster board – 3 pieces
2. Scissors & black marker pen
3. Large white trash bag and large black trash bag

Step 1:

Cut out 3 large footprints from the red poster board and write Repentance, Forgiveness and Restoration on the feet (one word on each foot). We chose a red board for these footprints to represent the blood of Jesus for without this, we would not have the privilege of repenting of our sins.

"If we confess our sins He is faithful and just to forgive us our sins and cleanse us from all unrighteousness."
1 John 1:9

Step 2:

Set up the following pattern on the floor. The black bag stands for sin and the white one stands for being cleansed so we are once again "white as snow."

Repentance   Forgiveness   Restoration

Step 3:

Write out scenarios of your kids' misbehaviors during the week. Pick a child and read a scenario for him to work through.

1. **Disobedience**: Have this child stand in the black "pit", telling him his heart is black because he has sinned (he didn't get his chores done). Ask him if he is ready to **repent** of his sin. If he says he is, he steps into the first footprint. If not, he sits in a chair with his hands folded until he is.

2. **Repentance:** Ask him to tell you **what** he did wrong (confession – I John 1:9) and if he is ready to make it right with you and God. Don't let him get off with saying "I did not obey." He needs to say **how** he did not obey ("I didn't do my chores because I was playing a game on the computer I wanted to finish.")

    ➢ Ask him what **heart attitude(s)** he violated–(he did not obey, he was not faithful, he did not have self-control)

    ➢ Ask him **how** he violated the **heart attitude(s)** – He did not **obey** by getting the chores done before dinner as he knew he should; He was not **faithful** by not doing them because you counted on them getting done; he didn't have the **self-control** to get the chores done instead of finishing the game.

    ➢ Ask him **why** what he did was wrong – Don't accept answers that aren't specific such as "The Bible says to be kind and I wasn't."
    *   The Bible says in Ephesians 6:1 and Colossians 3:23 kids are supposed to **obey** their parents and he didn't.
    *   He needs to tell you it was wrong to be unfaithful. He knew you counted on the chores getting done, especially setting the table for dinner and not

only did he let you down, you had to take time to do it yourself.

3. **Forgiveness**: He needs to *ask Jesus* to forgive him for not doing his chores and for letting you down.

   ➤ He needs to ask you for forgiveness, looking you in the eye.

4. **Restoration:** Your son needs to tell you how he is going to *make this right*. When you make something right, you replace what you did wrong with something good. He needed to tell you how he is going to work on putting the computer away the next time.

   ➤ Your son tells he will not start playing with the computer until his chores are done.

Note: *Restoration* is about making a relationship right; *restitution* is replacing material objects that were broken, taken away or destroyed.

5. **Cleansing**: Now your child has the freedom to step to the white 'pit' which means his heart is pure again.

"Though your sins are like scarlet, they shall be as white as snow."
Isaiah 1:18

"The next day he saw Jesus coming toward him and said,
'Behold the lamb of God who takes away the sin of the world.'"
John 1:29

While working through the "Repentance, Forgiveness and Restoration" process in this way takes time, it also is a **teacher**, showing your children they are accountable for their reactions to others. We know of teens and young adults whose parents used the footsteps to teach them how to work through this process when they were growing up who still talk about it. Your child's heart will never open up until he learns to seek forgiveness. Only then can we truly understand what God did for us.

> *"For God so loved the world that He gave His only Son,*
> *that whoever believes in Him should not perish but have eternal life.*
> *For God did not send His Son into the world to condemn the world,*
> *but in order that the world might be saved through Him."*
> John 3:16-17

Appendix B
Re-training a Stubborn Heart

Below is the chart referred to in Chapter 7. The best way to use this chart is:

- Make your own copy, putting just the first column down when you give it to your child to complete
- When your child has finished the first column, add the next column and give it back to him. Keep repeating this until all columns are filled
- For better understanding, please re-read Chapter 7

List All Sins Impacted by Your choice	**WHAT** Sin Did You Commit?	**WHO** Was Affected by Your Sin?	**HOW** Did Your Sin Affect Others?	**WHY** Did You Choose to Do It?	**HOW** Do you Need to Right This Wrong	**What** Will Change Now In You Now?

Appendix B

Bibliography

Chapter 1

1. Charles R. Swindoll, *Insight for Today Daily Devotionals,* "Sunday Listening, Part One," www.insightfortoday.org, July 5, 2014
2. Gary and Anne Marie Ezzo, *Growing Kids God's Way* (Louisiana, MO: Growing Families Int'l, 1988, 1992, 1997, 2002, 2007), 125-126.

Chapter 3

1. Merriam-Webster Online Dictionary, www.merriam-webster.com/dictionary/think Dictionary.com, dictionary.reference.com/browse/thinking

Chapter 5

1. Merriam-Webster Online Dictionary, www.merriam-webster.com/dictionary/think Dictionary.com, dictionary.reference.com/browse/thinking

2. Dictionary.Com Online Dictionary, www.dictionary.reference. com/browse/thinking

Chapter 6

1. *Making Brothers and Sisters Best Friends* by Sarah, Stephen and Grace Mally is a great book to read aloud as a family to learn to put siblings before self
2. Merriam-Webster Online Dictionary, www.merri-am-webster.com/dictionary/humble
3. President John F. Kennedy's Inaugural Address, January 20, 1961, www.ushistory.org/documents/ask-not.htm

Chapter 7

1. *Growing Up Christian* by Karl Graustein for Middle School age kids and *Own It* by Hayley DiMarco for older teens are great books about owning their faith
2. Alcoholic's Anonymous 12-Step Program, AA Step 5, www.recovery.com

Chapter 8

1. *Spirit-Controlled Temperaments* by Tim LaHaye is the best resource we have found to understand temperaments and their blends.
2. *The Treasure Tree* is a book written by Gary Smalley and John Trent that shares about four animals on an adventure. Ask your children which animal they think they are at the end of the story and you will most likely know what their primary temperament is. The lion is choleric, the otter is sanguine, the beaver is melancholy and the golden retriever is phlegmatic. You can find both of these books at www.parentingmadepractical.com.

Chapter 9

1. For more information on why you should expect your children to come to you at the call of his name you will want to get our book, *Why Can't I Get My Kids to Behave?*

Chapter 10

1. Gary and Anne Marie Ezzo, Growing Kids God's Way
   (Louisiana, MO: Growing Families Int'l, 1988, 1992, 1997,
   2002, 2007)

Chapter 12

1. Gary and Anne Marie Ezzo, Growing Kids God's Way
   (Louisiana, MO: Growing Families Int'l, 1988, 1992,
   1997, 2002

Resources by Joey and Carla Link

Study questions for each chapter of this book can be downloaded
at no charge at www.parentingmadepractical.com. Check this
website often for blogs on parenting topics by Joey and Carla Link.

Carla Link posts thoughts on parenting on the Parenting Made
Practical Facebook page several times a week. "Like" this page
and you will receive her posts on a regular basis.

Books and DVDs by Joey & Carla Link

➤ "Why Can't I Get My Kids to Behave?"–paperback, CD, MP3
➤ "Taming the Lecture Bug and Getting Your Kids to Think"–
  paperback, CD, MP3
➤ "Taming the Lecture Bug and Getting Your Kids to
  Think" DVD
➤ "Navigating the Rapids of Parenting" DVD helps parents
  pro-actively assist their kids as they go through age-ap-
  propriate transitions
➤ "Dating, Courting and Choosing a Mate – What Works?"
  DVD, Workbook, CD

The *Mom's Notes* Parenting Presentations

Over forty *Mom's Notes* teaching presentations on CD, MP3 and in written form can be purchased individually, in sets, Starter Packs of the most popular presentations or Volume Sets of eight presentations each.

The *Mom's Notes* share practical teaching on parenting topics for toddlers through the teen years. While the principle remains the same for all ages, the application will differ and is age-appropriate in its presentation.

Although both Joey and Carla wrote all the presentations, they are called *Mom's Notes* because for the most part Carla presented them to Mom's Groups across the country. By no means are these presentations intended for moms only.

Some of the most popular topics are:

- *"Understanding First-Time Obedience"*
- *"Discipline Issues."*
- *"It's All About Attitude"*
- *"Understanding Freedoms, Part 1* and *Part 2"*
- *"Understanding Character Training, Part 1* and *Part 2"*
- *"Training Toddlers"*
- *"Training Preschoolers"*
- *"Training Elementary School Age Children"*
- *"Training Middle School Age Children"*
- *"Building a Relationship of Trust with a Rebellious Teen"*
- *"Dealing with Sibling Conflict, Part 1* and *Part 2"*
- *"Parenting as Partners*
- On Temperaments – Working with Your Child's Besetting Sin: Part 1"*The Choleric: Training an Angry Child"*, Part 2 *"The Phelgmatic: Dealing with a Child Who is Stubborn and Unmotivated; The Sanguine: Working with the Child Who Lies"*, Part 3 *"The Melancholy: TeachingYour Child to Deal with His Emotions*

- Starter Pack for Children of All Ages (The 5 presentations we recommend all parents start with on CDs and Notes)
- Starter Pack for Toddlers and Preschoolers (The 6 presentations especially geared to this age group on CDs and Notes)
- Starter Pack for "Understanding First-Time Obedience"w/ laminated chart

All 40 presentations are at the
www.ParentingMadePractical.com bookstore

Parenting Resources
Recommended by Joey and Carla Link

To find out about *Growing Kids God's Way* and *Parenting from the Tree of Life* parenting classes, go to www.GFIUS.org.

BOOKS for PARENTS

- *On Becoming... Babywise, Toddlerwise, Preschoolwise, Childwise, Preteenwise,* and *Teenwise by* Gary Ezzo and Dr. Robert Bucknam
- *For Instruction in Righteousness by* Pam Forster
- *What Every Child Should Know Along the Way by* Gail Martin
- *No More Perfect Moms, No More Perfect Kids, Real Moms... Real Jesus* by Jill Savage
- *Set-Apart Motherhood* by Leslie Ludy
- *Parenting with Scripture* by Kara Durbin
- *Wisdom for Parents* by Frank Hamrick
- *Making Brothers and Sisters Best Friends* by Sarah Malley
- *Spirit-Controlled Temperaments* by Tim LaHaye
- *The Treasure Tree by Gary Smalley and John Tren*

BOOKS for TEENS

- ➤ *When God Writes Your Life Story, God's Gift to Women* by Eric Ludy
- ➤ *Set-Apart Femininity, Authentic Beauty* by Leslie Ludy
- ➤ *Set- Apart Girl* online magazine by Leslie Ludy
- ➤ *A Young Man After God's Own Heart, A Young Man's Guide to Making Right Choices* by Jim George
- ➤ *A Young Woman After God's Own Heart, A Young Woman's Guide to Making Right Choices* by Elizabeth George
- ➤ *Die Young, God Girl, Devotions for the God Girl* by Hayley DiMarco
- ➤ *Die Young, God Guy, Devotions for the God Guy* by Michael DiMarco
- ➤ *7 Steps to Knowing, Doing and Experiencing the Will of God for Teens* by Tom Blackaby
- ➤ *Girls Gone Wise in a World Gone Wild* by Mary Kassian
- ➤ *How to Give Away Your Faith, Know What You Believe* by Paul Little

**You will find these and over 200 books at
parentingmadepractical.com**

About the Authors

*J*oey and Carla Link are parent educators who are known for making parenting practical, thus the name Parenting Made Practical. Joey served for 16 years as the youth and/or family pastor at three different churches in Southern California and Iowa. He enjoys revisiting his youth pastor days when he has the opportunity to speak and teach to teens at teen conferences and camps.

For over 20 years Joey has been the Director of Family Life Resources, a non-profit ministry to families with the mission to "provide biblical resources to churches, Christian organizations and individuals and to assist parents in discipling their children in order to raise a godly generation." The Links have partnered with Growing Families Int'l, an international parenting ministry for over 20 years as well.

Carla's degree is in social work. She has assisted Joey in whatever ministry he has served in by writing and teaching Bible Studies for pre-teen and teenage girls and college-age and adult women. She is a popular speaker for GEMS, MOPS, Mom to Mom and other groups for moms, as well as co-teaching with Joey at parenting conferences.

Joey and Carla travel extensively across the country teaching and speaking at churches, parenting conferences and seminars. Together, they bring a unique and fresh blend of teaching to parents. The Links live in Burlington, Iowa and have three grown children and two grandchildren.

Would you like to hear more of their teaching?

Contact Joey and Carla about speaking at your church, parenting conference, seminar, community parenting event, homeschool function, Mom's group and/or teen conference at

www.parentingmadepractical.com